ANALYSING LEARNING NEEDS

To my wife Margaret
for all her efforts in checking and giving encouragement
throughout the writing of this first book,
and to
Alison and Andrew
for their support.

Analysing learning needs

Malcolm Craig, PhD

Consultant editor: Billie Taylor
of the Nottingham Trent University

Gower

© Malcolm Craig 1994

Published by
Gower Publishing Limited
Gower House
Croft Road
Aldershot
Hampshire GU11 3HR
England

Gower
Old Post Road
Brookfield
Vermont 05036
USA

British Library Cataloguing in Publication Data
Craig, Malcolm
    Analysing Learning Needs
    I. Title
    658.3124

ISBN 0–566–07448–6 ✓

Library of Congress Cataloging-in-Publication Data
Craig, Malcolm
    Analyzing learning needs / Malcolm Craig.
        p. cm.
    Includes bibliographical references and index.
ISBN 0–566–07448–6 : $54.95 (est.)
    1. Employees—Training of. 2. Needs assessment.
HF5549.5.T7C68 1994
658.3'12404—dc20   94–9677
                                                                    CIP

Typeset in 11 point Palatino by Bournemouth Colour Graphics Limited, Parkstone, Dorset and printed in Great Britain by the University Press, Cambridge.

Contents

Figures and tables

Figures

Tables

Preface

This book is designed for a wide range of people, in both industry and education, who are directly or indirectly involved in helping people to learn in the workplace. These will typically be managers, supervisors and trainers in the office or on the shop floor, and tutors or lecturers on educational courses related to employment.

The main benefits to be derived from applying the ideas and techniques presented in this book are as follows:

- An increased capacity to identify learning needs in less conventional working conditions.
- An increased awareness that in a rapidly changing workplace it is more important to have a strategy that can be applied flexibly to the identification of learning need than to rely on one favourite method.
- To enable managers, supervisors and trainers to *plan* for learning needs, instead of reacting to such needs.
- To help reduce the gap between the introduction of new technologies and their full utilization by skilled people.
- To target quickly, prime areas where skills and knowledge are needed.
- For managers, supervisors and trainers to demonstrate a deeper understanding of different skill and knowledge types and how these are learned.

The underlying purpose of this book is to encourage people to look beyond the common check-list approach to training needs analysis which assumes that organizational life is clearly bounded and fairly static. It is my contention that people working in this area are now required to adopt a more imaginative view of this subject.

Our working lives are changing significantly, and therefore our ideas about analysing people's training needs should change accordingly. The idea that one method can serve to analyse the varied skills which more flexible working arrangements demand, seems difficult to justify. It is clear that a holistic treatment of training needs analysis is now required. In this book I examine changing working patterns and changing relationships between skills, and link these changes to a new approach to analysing changing needs.

When we explore the factors that cause us to question how support is given for learning at work we discover that it is learning support that is critical rather than training. In other words, people can be helped to learn in ways other than what we commonly think of as 'training'. While training can play a large part in people's learning opportunity, it is more helpful, at the needs identification stage, to focus upon learning needs. Moreover this terminology fits in with the idea of lifelong learning; given that occupational learning is for life, then analysing learning needs is for life. The half-life of a technical person's learning is now five years, that is, half of what has been learned during any one block of learning will be obsolete in five years. This book therefore concentrates on the analysis of learning needs rather than training needs.

Most chapters of the book include a self-diagnosis section to help you check your current level of understanding against the contents of the chapter. The material has been structured in a way that encourages you to relate the ideas and techniques to your own experience, so it is best to allow time for reflection between readings of the sections.

A number of techniques have been introduced; you can choose those that are most appropriate to your situation. In all cases there is more information available than can be fitted into the scope of this book and for that reason full references have been supplied, together with a list of further reading.

I trust that some or all of the material will be of value to you in your work.

Malcolm Craig

1 Patterns of new work practices

Background

The past twenty years have seen dramatic changes in the types of work that people are called upon to do and corresponding changes in the skills, knowledge and abilities required. An event that contributed most to these changes was the invention of the microprocessor in 1971. This innovation triggered other technological developments which resulted in many jobs becoming obsolete or changing, an effect which has been felt in manufacturing, service and finance areas of employment. During the post-war years up to the 1970s people organized their working lives in a relatively stable manner, but now the trend is towards greater flexibility in working practices and for many people this means living with uncertainty. The effect of these changes is not confined to any one section of the working population; new knowledge, skills and ability needs can extend throughout a workforce, starting at senior director level. Many types of support are needed to help people cope with the problematic and at times disruptive circumstances which result. As personal relationships and the use of skills and knowledge requirements change people may feel that they are losing control over their working lives. A theme of this book is that one method of giving people helpful support is to increase access to appropriate learning but first what has to be learned must be clearly analysed. Throughout this book I refer to this as the analysis of learning needs.

The most common approach to the subject of knowledge and skills identification at work has been training needs analysis. This approach assumes that the analysis method is appropriate for most areas of employment and most jobs. When job functions and patterns of working were more stable, during the 1960s and earlier, it was possible to prescribe with some confidence a method for analysis of this kind. The outcome is normally a 'recipe-book' approach to the analysis of training needs. A further assumption of the approach is that most work-based learning can be satisfied by training.

The term 'training needs analysis' can be seen as a contradiction, because the analysis is made in anticipation that training will be needed. If, from the beginning, the focus of any analysis is upon training then it follows that the outcome will be that a training need either does or does not exist. When, instead, the emphasis is on the kind of support people need in order to learn and to adapt to fresh circumstances, a different outcome will be achieved. Thus, people who are responsible for analysing training needs must now take account of a number of varied needs that are related to the process of learning at work.

An important premise of the training needs analysis approach is that people work for large-, medium- or small-sized organizations for approximately forty hours each week and perform within a hierarchy that can readily be described with the aid of a traditional organization chart. In addition it is assumed that training resources are accessible to those with training needs. While this fairly stable and predictable situation still exists in many companies, significant developments are steadily changing once familiar work patterns.

One of the most important developments is a move towards smaller core groups of people within organizations who are supported by people on the periphery of these organizations. People at the periphery are generally expected to work in a more flexible way. One of the main reasons suggested for this move to core-group working is that uncertainty in the market place can be accommodated by employing on a contract basis as demand dictates. The kind of support for learning that people need on the periphery of organizations has not been fully explored and areas of learning need also exist for those who remain at the core of organizations, to help them cope with changing relationships as other people move to the periphery. As this trend continues, the number of people who share their working time between more than one organization will increase and they will have learning needs that may not always be easily identified, or which might even be in conflict when they have been identified.

The most prominent sign of a shift to the periphery of organizations is the increase in home-based working. In some cases work is shared between an organization base and the home, in others the home is the base for full-time employment with an employer. Some people are home-based and independent. Whatever the particular working arrangement, real learning needs do arise. The prime aim of any analysis of learning need is to anticipate and to target the necessary support in advance of any knowledge or skills need at work. For people working at home this aim can be particularly difficult to achieve. A system of analysis to identify needs in remote situations has to be sensitive to a number of factors, and for this reason a theme of this book is that more than one technique can be used to provide a more sensitive analysis.

Another development in work patterns is the shift in balance between the number of younger and older people in the labour market. The change to a greater proportion of older people means that appropriate support is needed, particularly to help them learn new skills and knowledge more easily. Extensive research over the past forty years that points the way to most effective learning for the older person and, where appropriate, significant points from this research will be highlighted in the book to give some direction to the identification of learning needs in this area. Other sections of the labour market may also require particular attention. The increase in the number of one-parent families suggests that the learning needs of these parents in either full or part-time work should be considered. Qualitative differences may be apparent in the kinds of learning needs and support for learning that they require. As the way people are employed becomes more fluid and unpredictable, important implications for people with disabilities can be seen. Such people need appropriate learning support to help them adapt to changing work practices.

The adoption of various forms of new technology and workplace design has led to new types of injury and illness. An important question here is how far learning can contribute to the avoidance of such injury. A standard method of training needs analysis is inadequate for the task of identifying needs in the area of injury avoidance. What is required is an ergonomic-based technique to discover what, if any, type of learning will contribute to the avoidance of injury.

A broader view of changes in work patterns reveals a significant shift in the use of skills. The most obvious shift has been from skilled, semi-skilled and unskilled manual work to a wider use of thinking or cognitive skills. Typical cognitive skills are reasoning, problem-solving, sequencing of a process, decision-making and creative working. As this change has occurred people in mid-to-late working life have been called upon to learn skills that have not been tapped since they were in full-time education.

The general move towards greater use of cognitive skills raises a number of issues for people whose task it is to analyse training needs or identify learning needs. One issue is how to cope with the 'shelf-life' of a skill. Many of the traditional manual or motor skills were learned and perfected to a point where they had permanence or a very long shelf-life. Filing metal, bricklaying and riding a bicycle are skills that are readily recognizable as being of this kind. On the other hand, many cognitive skills have a very short shelf-life unless they have been learned in a particular way and even then they can be lost if not reinforced by practice on the actual job. The skills of computer numerical controlled machine tool programming, networking and information processing typically spring to mind. Another issue that arises from the shift to cognitive skills is whether some young school-leavers are adequately prepared for the learning of cognitive skills that, at times, demand significant levels of conceptual reasoning. Evidence suggests that many young people in industrialized countries are less than fully prepared to meet the challenge of learning work-based cognitive skills. The entry point into any learning programme at work has to include a statement about prerequisites that are needed before effective learning can begin. Other issues relevant to the shift towards more cognitive skills use will be discussed at appropriate places in the book.

In addition to the many changes in work patterns significant developments in technology have allowed people to learn more easily and there is a wider range of learning methods to cater for different needs. Large numbers of people in industry are unaware of much of this development; learning is regarded as a process of formal training delivered in the form of a course either on or off the job. It could be argued that any analysis of learning needs must be accompanied by adequate information about the learning support that is currently available; the two are interactive. If, for example, learning needs are being analysed because a new process is being introduced, it is possible that little or no learning support is available. Appropriate aids to learning would therefore need to be developed alongside the analysis of needs.

Developing a strategy

Flexible and increasingly complex approaches to work and skill use demand a strategy for the analysis of learning needs rather than a rigid method. This strategy comprises a toolbox of techniques from which one or more techniques can be selected and used to provide support for people who need to learn new skills and knowledge (see Figure 1.1). So that the techniques can be used effectively this book also includes information about various types of skill and about the various abilities that are used in learning a particular skill; without a thorough understanding in this area it is difficult to respond effectively to developments in technology. A more detailed description of skills and abilities and how they are related is given in the next chapter.

Figure 1.1 lists the techniques in the order that they are introduced in the book. In Chapters 4 and 5 the techniques are covered in a 'how to' form with practical examples of typical application in the workplace.

An effective strategy for the analysis of learning needs, as described in this book, should include the following elements:

- A way to describe the target situation where needs can exist.
- An open mind about what the use of techniques may reveal about the learning needs.
- Familiarity with three or four techniques that are most suitable in your situation.
- The means of choosing one or more appropriate techniques.
- An open effective channel of communication with everyone involved.
- The means of anticipating learning needs from an investigation of business plans.

Information gathering
Listening and questioning
Critical incident technique (CIT)
Trainability
Brainstorming/Brainwriting
Survey questionnaire

Analysis
Force field
Delphi
Job analysis
Abilities approach
AET
Protocol analysis
Repertory grid
Skills analysis
SWOT
Nominal group
Cartoon story board

Figure 1.1   Investigative techniques

The strategy needs to be part of a continuous process and from time to time it may be necessary to discount some techniques and adopt others as skill requirements and working practices change. In other words, the method of analysis that you adopt must be flexible enough to match the flexibility of future work patterns.

From office to home

The movement of people from office-based to home-based work has already taken place in a number of organizations and in some cases the move has been towards almost total home working. If the trend continues we will have to review what is meant by the term 'organization', but meanwhile the joint learning needs of two categories of people must be considered. On the one hand there are those who remain office-based and whose working relationships are changed by the shift in work patterns of colleagues. Then there are the needs of people who 'move out'; in their case it is important that analysis of learning needs forms part of the preparation for a change in work patterns.

To help satisfy the technical, logistical or back-up needs of people who now work from home, 'tele-cottages' (small business centres, where information technology equipment is provided for the use of independent workers on a 'club' type arrangement) have been introduced from Scandinavia. An analysis of learning needs has to take account of such developments, for example, what particular skills and knowledge, if any, are required before people can fully exploit additional sources of technology near the home?

If you work from home independently are you sustained by the skills and knowledge acquired when you were based in an organization? If so, what is the shelf-life of these skills and knowledge? What means are available for anticipating future skills and knowledge needs and how is the learning associated with such needs to be identified? A number of such questions can be generated and each one points to an issue that is linked to changing work patterns between the traditional organization and the home. It is impossible here to explore all issues of this kind but those issues where the analysis of learning needs becomes critical and where a different approach to analysing learning needs is required will be highlighted.

From motor skills to cognitive skills

The aim of this section is to provide an overview of how the use of skills in the workplace is changing. The most important part of such an overview is to provide a range of different examples of how change is taking place, and then to look for lessons that can be drawn as a result of making a comparison between them. An important issue is the implications of these changes for people and in particular their need for continuous learning. When you have read some of these examples, think of your own workplace, or one that is of particular interest to you such as a hospital, bank, factory or consultancy practice, and assess how far such developments have taken place, where they have taken place, and what has been done to provide support for learning.

In the nineteenth century most work was conveniently divided between 'doers' and 'thinkers'. On the doing side, where mainly motor skills were used, were a wide range of highly skilled jobs such as shipwright, printer, turner, coppersmith and blacksmith. Most of these jobs are now obsolete or in serious decline. The semi-skilled to unskilled jobs, such as capstan operator, machine minder, shop assistant, servant or cleaner used lower level motor skills and with only a few exceptions have remained largely unchanged (the functions performed by servants are now represented by other job titles associated with the service industry). While highly skilled physical jobs have become obsolete or gone into serious decline, the semi-skilled and unskilled physical jobs have simply reduced in number. For tasks that involve mainly thinking, where cognitive skills are used, jobs such as manager, foreman, clerk, lawyer and teacher have in contrast remained largely intact. Over the past twenty years a steady growth has occurred in new jobs such as systems analyst, knowledge engineer, corporate manager, network engineer and consultants of various kinds. The kind of new job that provides people with a career tends to be strongly biased towards the use of cognitive skills.

In addition to the growth in cognitive skill use, the dividing line between the use of motor skills and cognitive skills has blurred. The merging of motor and cognitive skills is apparent in the practical examples given in the case study section which follows. Fewer jobs contain predominantly motor skills and usually include chunks of cognitive skills too. The mixing of skill types has increasingly presented a problem for traditional methods of training needs analysis because the different types of skill interact and can no longer be viewed separately.

The 'thinking' jobs of the past have not avoided the changes generated by 1970s' technology; skill types have not been mixed, but changes have occurred in the way that cognitive skill is applied in the workplace. A stronger emphasis has developed on troubleshooting, personal relations, creativity, innovation and planning.

In general, in western industrialized countries an unmistakable move has been made towards the development of higher value-added goods that require creativity, innovation, and forecasting in their development, and higher levels of cognitive skill use in their production. The strong innovative aspect of work suggests that some of the cognitive skills being learned may have a short shelf-life and it is for this reason, more than any other, that learning to learn should now be a priority in schools and should be matched by adequate support for learning throughout working life.

Case studies

This section covers a range of different work settings and gives practical examples of how work patterns are changing and how in turn there are associated changes to the use of knowledge and skills.

Textile workers

Before the introduction of microprocessor control of weaving looms, a weaver's task was to operate a loom as effectively as possible. The motor skills used involved a high level dexterity of hand and finger manipulation. Since the introduction of semi-automated looms a weaver has been able to control a number of looms. The effective weaver is now the person who can exercise a high level of cognitive skill in the form of reasoning, sequencing and troubleshooting. This task can be likened to keeping balls in the air: making rapid choices between actions to be taken on one loom rather than another. The result is that the most effective weavers, in terms of output, actually expend less physical effort because their superior cognitive-based strategy allows them to control the looms in a relaxed way. The identification of learning needs for weavers who do not have an effective strategy can be problematic, because those weavers who have developed an effective strategy often find it difficult to articulate the skills being used. Three techniques in particular have proved to be useful: protocol analysis, simulation and critical incident. When the skills to be learned have been identified the support can be provided in the form of simulation-based training, by self-directed assimilation of the necessary skill or by shadowing a more effective weaver.

Health workers with the mentally ill

In the last decade in the United Kingdom changes have been made in the care of the mentally ill. Briefly, a move has occurred from care within large institutions to care within the community. The various types of support needed by the mentally ill require much thought and planning, but support is also needed for the staff who previously cared for them in the institutions. The term 'institutionalized' is more often applied to patients, but it can also apply to staff who have spent some years working in this way. Such institutions provided secure, stable working conditions for staff and most of the help they needed was readily available. The main skills in use were linked to organization, care and various forms of personal relationships.

A move to community-based care has many implications for the use of skills by the staff, one of the most significant of which is increased autonomy and independence in making decisions. Some strong similarities can be seen here with people who are moving from organization to home-based working; people can become institutionalized in companies too. Other implications arise from the need to liaise with a range of different people and to draw upon information from different sources. What staff need to learn in order to facilitate this kind of change effectively needs to be identified. Such techniques as delphi, storyboard or force field can help to identify the type of learning support required.

Printers

For five hundred years, up to the introduction of the microprocessor, printing developed in a way that required a high level of motor skill. This skilled job was fully mastered only after serving a seven-year apprenticeship. Now the skill is virtually obsolete and periodicals, books and newspapers can be transferred directly from the computer screen to the printing press. The high level motor skill has been replaced, almost entirely, by cognitive skills. The skills used now are linked to monitoring, problem-solving, decision-making and sequencing of operations. A problem in identifying learning need is that the technology is relatively new to the area of work and there is no 'history' of effective practices to draw upon. Finding out exactly what needs to be learned requires a strategy that can cover both an overview of a complex machine system and the finer detail of how the technology functions. Where new applications of technology are involved, one or more of the investigative techniques should be used with whoever can provide insight into the technology. In this case, the critical incident technique has proved to be the most valuable, but others such as simulation and structured observation have also proved to be effective.

Branch bank managers

Recent developments in the operation of local banks have led to changes in the use of skills by the manager. This case study illustrates changes in the use of cognitive skills rather than a shift from motor skill to cognitive, as described above. For many years, up to the 1980s, most work conducted in the branches of banks was well-ordered, stable and to a large extent predictable; for both managers and staff there was security of employment that appeared to be permanent. However, this security in employment has been lost, largely as a result of the introduction of the microprocessor and the attendant growth in information technology. For managers, changes in the use of their skills have been brought about mainly by the diversification of services offered by banks. Each manager must now be more pro-active and able to make decisions about a range of clients and businesses. Where branches have closed managers have had to adapt to a corporate manager role, within larger centres of a bank.

The implications of these changes for learning needs are considerable. The pace of technological development has been so rapid that managers may not be sufficiently aware of the implications to be able to ask meaningful questions about what support is available. The use of investigative techniques can be particularly valuable in helping managers to frame significant questions as a first step in identifying needs.

The skill–use issue can be further complicated by the influence of personality types upon the planned changes. Certain personality types are generally attracted to jobs where security and stability are essential aspects of the work. When suddenly the work becomes unpredictable and flexible the difficulty in adapting can cloud the task of learning what needs to be learned. Thus a deeper understanding of cognitive skills and in particular an awareness of how human abilities influence changes between types of cognitive skill is required. The abilities approach technique is particularly suited to this purpose. The staff in banks largely share the work pattern changes with their managers and must learn to adapt to a form of work that was not anticipated when they joined the organization. Many of the changes involve relationships, so the repertory grid technique and force field are useful options.

Multi-discipline team-building

This case study shows how learning needs can arise from a development that changes the relationship between skills and how they are used. The technique of training needs analysis can be used with architects, designers, engineers or planners as they perform the various tasks within these roles and this has been the approach in the past. Recent changes in work patterns, however, have led to a much closer grouping of the roles into project teams. Each team is multi-disciplined and is led by someone who is not necessarily the direct manager of people in the team. In other words the team members report to a manager but are managed by the team leader for the duration of the project. Multi-discipline teams in which people work closely together are becoming increasingly common, usually for one-off projects. Being part of such a team affects the use of skill not only when in the team but also when dealing with a parent department. Quite important implications for learning exist for the team leader/manager, team members and for the managers of team members who operate outside the team.

This example of a changing work pattern illustrates well how working practices can become more complex, revealing a complicated interaction between the learning needs of the team and those of individuals both inside and outside the team. This leads in turn to a search for a strategy that can deal with three sets of need while maintaining an overview of the wider work situation. Such a strategy ought to include critical incident and delphi techniques in that order. It should be possible to contain all necessary learning support within the team but outside learning support may also be required.

Single parents in employment

This is not the place to discuss the wider implications of single parents in employment, but we should be aware of the growth in single-parenting either by choice or necessity. It is clear that the number of such parents in the workplace will grow. On the one hand, single parents may find current developments in working practices acting in their favour, that is, the increased use of flexible working on a contract basis. On the other hand, however, they may suffer along with many other 'peripheral' working people and receive inadequate learning support. The main question to be asked is whether single parents in either full-time or part-time employment experience learning needs differently to other employees who do not have the added demands of single-parenthood. Such analysis recognizes that while people generally prefer to keep their working lives and domestic lives separate there is an inescapable two-way influence between work and family life.

The issue is of relevance to personnel professionals in large organizations and managers in small- to medium-sized organizations. A strategy is needed to explore whether employees in this category, including directors as well as other members of a company, have adequate learning support and whether this varies in any way to the needs of others. It is possible to take advantage of the flexibility offered by a multi-technique approach to learning needs analysis and ask such people to work through one or two techniques of brainwriting, SWOT and/or storyboard to highlight needs, initially for skills and knowledge, and then for learning.

People with disabilities

There is a need to have a clear picture of the implications arising from the introduction of new technology upon people who have disabilities. If appropriate learning can help them to adapt to new working practices a whole new range of opportunities can be opened up, but if appropriate learning support cannot be identified the opportunities in the labour market will continue to shrink. We all have disabilities in that some of our abilities are weak or hardly function at all, but in terms of the complex competitive workplace some people have more handicapping disabilities than others.

As technology develops we need to identify what type of learning support is required by people who otherwise might be excluded from finding fulfilling occupations. Although it is preferable to integrate people with disabilities fully into the standard workplace, some organizations are able specifically to accommodate the needs of people with disabilities. Such organizations provide a valuable service either as long-term employers or as a stepping stone to other forms of work. However, changes in working practice may lead to people with more severe disabilities being excluded from what has become a more competitive working environment. Wherever possible, ways need to be found to provide the vital learning support needed by people with disabilities; with adequate support they can achieve far more than may commonly be believed possible. The most important requirement in approaching the analysis of learning needs in this area is an open mind; stereotyping people with disabilities has to be avoided. Investigative techniques can help people with disabilities to explore their potential in the new and developing market place for jobs. The techniques of particular value are nominal group, SWOT, trainability and structured observation.

Older workers

Demographic changes, due to the lower birth rate in developed industrialized countries, will lead to a greater proportion of older people in the workforce. Older people will have the opportunity to learn new skills and knowledge to compensate for the decline in numbers of younger people coming into the labour market, but how well can older people learn in terms of the time required and eventual level of achievement? Although motor and cognitive abilities decline with age, there is as much within-age difference as there is between ages of young and old when comparisons are made; some older people have more effective motor and cognitive abilities than some younger people. When appropriate learning is applied few differences are apparent across the age ranges, as the Open University can demonstrate with students aged from 20 to 80 years old. For people who wish to continue to contribute to the workplace a change of skill use or even career ought to be possible at any age and learning support should be available for this purpose.

A strategy for the analysis of learning needs has to be sensitive to what is meant by abilities and how abilities transfer between different occupations. Some older people when faced with the task of learning a new skill or set of knowledge adopt a 'blank-page' approach and start their learning from scratch. An awareness of their abilities can lead them to realize that possibly 50 per cent or more of the required learning has already been achieved. Some learning for older people is little more than a topping-up exercise. A further factor to be taken into account is that the type of learning support chosen can either help or hinder learning for the older person; years of research have led to recommended approaches to learning for the upper age-group but they appear to have had little impact. Managers from various organizations can still be heard to justify age limits on recruitment by saying that older people are incapable of learning new skills and knowledge. In the next few years organizations will have to take more account of approaches to learning for the older worker.

Summary

The general aim of this chapter has been to provide a broad overview of changes in patterns of work and to highlight some of the implications for training needs analysis. Part of the overview has emphasized a shift, over the past twenty years, from relatively stable ways of working to more complex and unpredictable forms of employment. People are adjusting to these changes with varying degrees of success. One factor that enables some people to benefit from these changes is the opportunity they have for learning, whether self-directed through distance learning methods, or by being fortunate enough to work for an organization that values continued learning. In some cases, learning opportunity has been restricted through a lack of adequate information transfer in a company, a lack of training or a lack of facilities for self-directed learning. In such cases employees have tended to become more vulnerable in the face of changing technology. Generally, a lack of organizational learning exists because no strategy was in place to allow it to happen.

As technology develops at a rapid rate, some managers are not always in a position to ask meaningful questions about what needs to be learned. A typical reaction is to buy in a training programme that appears to correspond to what is happening. The outcome is training based upon course availability, one of the worst forms of training available to a company. A manager wishing to respond flexibly to ever changing demands on skills and knowledge needs a strategy for analysing learning needs, rather than a set method.

2 Skills, knowledge and abilities

Self-diagnosis

What is your understanding of skills, knowledge and abilities? The aim of this section is to make you begin asking yourself questions about how people learn skills and associated knowledge and how human abilities influence learning.

First, look at the list of terms in Figure 2.1 and think about what they mean to you. Imagine that you are going to describe the terms to a friend who knows little about education or training. A good idea, if you have the time, is to write a few lines of description for each term.

- Learning
- Education
- Training
- Skill
- Abilities
- Mentoring

- Discovery learning
- Simulation
- Self-directed learning
- Open learning
- Distance learning

Figure 2.1 Some training and education terms

When you have given some thought to this, consider the degree of linkage between the terms as you generally make use of them: are they all closely linked or do some represent parts of working life that are kept quite separate? Also, what would you say, looking at Figure 2.1, are the most common methods used by people when they need to learn new skills and knowledge? Are there any skills, or use of knowledge, that some people never seem to master completely? If the answer to this last question is yes, what explanations are commonly given for the gap between what they need to do and what they are able to do? In addition to thinking about these questions in relation to other people, think also of your own reactions to the learning of skills and knowledge. What are the most common explanations you use to assess your success or lack of success in learning? Without some understanding of what can help or hinder our own and other people's learning it becomes quite difficult to identify what is needed to support learning in general.

When you have completed this self-diagnosis of what you understand about learning, study the section below, as well as definitions of the various terms used in the book, examples of various behaviours that can be critical to learning are discussed.

Background

A number of key terms are used throughout the book, most of which are contained in Figure 2.2 (p. 16). The terms are defined below as they are applied in the context of this book.

Learning

A change in behaviour. Without a change in verbal and/or non-verbal behaviour it is not possible to know whether learning has taken place. The learning may be effective, ineffective, good, poor, harmful or supportive but for it to have occurred at all there must be a change in behaviour.

Education

An assimilation of knowledge, understanding, awareness and skills that is designed to provide a permanent personal resource and basis for future scholarship.

Training

Job-related assimilation of knowledge, understanding, awareness and skill that is designed for immediate use to facilitate performance of a specific task and which must have rapid reinforcement through practice on the actual job. The function of training cannot be expected to provide skills and knowledge for some future use, this is the role of education.

Skill

A precise activity that requires both learning and practice for its complete fulfilment. There are three types of skill: cognitive, motor and perceptual. Skill is most commonly thought of in relation to manual jobs but the meaning is much broader; people such as nurses, police officers, judges, accountants and hairdressers all practise skills of various kinds.

Abilities

The innate capacity of human beings to learn and practise skills and knowledge. Examples of abilities are colour discrimination, visualization, finger dexterity, multi-limb coordination and inductive reasoning. Some abilities can be improved with learning and practice, but others are difficult if not impossible to improve, given the current level of learning technology. The use of our abilities has a significant influence upon how we learn.

Mentoring

The care for learning and development shown by one person towards another which is achieved mainly through a spontaneous coming together. Attempts to structure the approach and make it happen means that the essence of mentoring is lost.

Discovery learning

A means of learning that relies upon exploration through searching and structured observation. It can be an effective approach to learning in situations where no possible hazards can exist.

Simulation

The reproduction of real-life events in model form to allow for repeated learning and practice in situations where this would otherwise be difficult or impossible.

Self-directed learning

A flexible approach to the assimilation of knowledge, understanding, awareness and skill that can be applied either for immediate use or conducted in a way that provides for long-term need. It draws upon appropriate support for learning, such as open and distance learning methods.

Open learning

The presentation of material, whether text, computer-based, multimedia, simulation or audio-visual, in a way that allows total freedom in how people choose to plan their learning. Open learning requires tutor support and can be conducted in a class, at work or individually at a distance.

Distance learning

The use of any form of learning but at a distance from the place of work or centre of learning. The terms shown in Figure 2.2 are the main ones that link learning needs to skills, knowledge and abilities through the different types of support. The term 'self-directed learning' also covers discovery, open and distance approaches.

At this point you may like to reflect upon your responses to the self-diagnostic section and check how close or how far apart these were when compared with the definitions given here. It is important to understand what these key words mean throughout the text, even if you disagree with my definitions; it does help, of course, if there is some shared understanding.

The general aim of this chapter is to explore skills, knowledge and abilities in the context of changing work patterns, to provide knowledge to support a strategy for analysing learning needs.

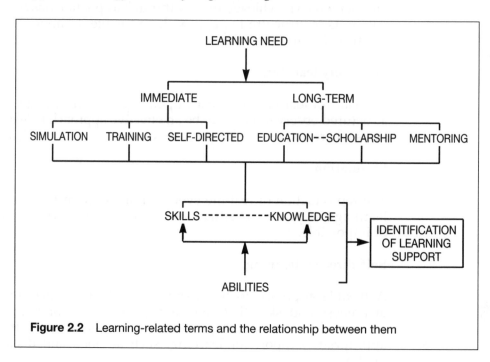

Figure 2.2   Learning-related terms and the relationship between them

Types of skill

Skill, and how different people exercise it, can be a fascinating subject for study. For example, in the learning of skill, what allows a ballet dancer, football player or boxer to achieve peak performance? How much common ground is there between the skills used in these three occupations? In each case is predominantly one type of skill used, or is there a complex mix of different types? Can *anyone* achieve peak performance given the most effective learning support or do abilities determine the eventual outcome? The knowledge and understanding necessary to answer such questions are still quite limited and as a result few people realize their full potential. One of the consequences of new technology is that the time required to learn specific work-based skills has been reduced to weeks and months, as opposed to the years associated with more traditional ways of working. The main implication of this is that people can expect to learn a large number of skills in a few years, possibly within two or more different jobs.

To understand skill a little better let us examine the three types of skill. When you have read this section you should be able to recognize types of skill being used when you see a person at work or a sportsperson at play. With a little more thought and familiarity with the make-up of skills you will also be able to identify which type of skill is likely to be most vital to performance.

Cognitive skill

Cognitive skill covers all skilled activity that could be described as 'thinking'. Playing chess, discovering the fault in a broken-down car or deciding to spend millions of pounds in a property deal are extreme examples of cognitive skill use.

Do not confuse cognitive skill use with knowledge use; knowledge, as described later, is now like water on tap and probably the most important knowledge concerns where to find knowledge. Cognitive skill use on the other hand is about how we process this knowledge in our daily tasks at home and at work. One of the most important aspects of dealing with fast changing technologies is how we conceptualize the new ideas around us and so recognize the common threads which run through many of the tasks performed at work. This recognition can enable people to transfer more readily between different jobs. However, to operate at this level people need to develop their cognitive skills.

Perceptual skill

Perceptual skill is concerned with seeing and interpreting what we see. The witness who gives police an accurate description of a person after only a brief sighting is exercising strong perceptual skill; there is a wide range of skilled performance among people in this respect, as the police know only too well. A power station controller who scans a large instrument panel and is confident that all is well, or that a problem is likely to occur, is also using perceptual skill. A further example of this type of skill is when a hairdresser matches a particular style to a client's features to the satisfaction of everyone.

The development of computer graphics has had an impact upon how this type of skill can be exercised. Certain perceptual skills, like some cognitive skills, can have a short shelf-life. A good example of this is when someone who has been using spanners in a skilled way ceases to practise the skill for some time. When skilled, the person could select the correct spanner at the first attempt with only a glance – an illustration of a strong perceptual skill. After some time without practising the skill, the person finds that a few spanners have to be tried before the correct one is found. In planning for learning needs it cannot be assumed that because someone has performed a skill in the past that skilled performance can be quickly revived. This applies in particular to cognitive and perceptual skills.

Motor skill

This type of skill involves doing, and covers all human physical movement. Driving a motor vehicle involves multi-limb coordination in quite a complex way. A dentist uses fine hand and finger manipulation, together with gross body orientation, when performing the necessary motor skills. The actual motor skills used by the dentist are similar to those used by a hairdresser and a surgeon to perform their tasks. Motor skills take many forms such as finger dexterity, upper limb control, hand–eye coordination and fine wrist movement. Most motor skills require well structured learning that is closely related to the task in hand; ballet dancers, dentists, motor mechanics, potters and farriers all make use of job-related learning. Motor skills cannot be learnt well on training programmes that are divorced from actual places of work. When planning for motor-skill learning needs, remember that such learning has to be reinforced with job-related practice immediately following the learning period. If this does not happen, you will have wasted time and money.

While it is enormously helpful to think of skill use as being of three kinds, in practice considerable overlap often exists between types of skill. During any analysis of learning needs questions should be asked about such overlap: how far does it exist and can the learning needs be confined to only one type of skill?

Linking types of skill

Skills often 'mesh' together in the performance of a job. The work of a dentist provides a good example of skill meshing: high level motor skills are combined with acute perceptual skill and the cognitive skill of reasoning and decision-making. We can all think of similar jobs that fit this description. Some jobs involve only two types of skill; the lawyer, senior manager and referee use perceptual and cognitive skills but no motor skill. The accountant and writer use cognitive skills almost exclusively. Where there is a complex meshing of all three types of skill it is possible to identify one skill type that is more important to job performance than any other.

In cases where such discrimination between skill types is not possible much thought should be given to the analysis of learning needs and to how different kinds of learning support can be provided. Should learning be conducted in a broad holistic way with skill types in tandem or should skill types be broken down so that learning can take place by building brick-by-brick, sometimes known as part-learning? The identification of skill types is also important to enable them to be matched to the various options for learning support.

One such option is distance learning, which can serve the needs of cognitive skills very well. However, distance learning is not so useful where perceptual skill is important such as in personal relationships, or in the practice of motor skill where it may be difficult to receive immediate feedback. On the other hand, simulation is particularly valuable to aid the learning of perceptual skill, such as practised by the power station controller. The cost of simulation techniques may well be justified in this instance but the approach may not be so effective in the learning of cognitive skill unless a strong tutor type back-up is provided to help with any reasoning, planning or decision-making. Similar comments apply to open learning support. Without tutor back-up it is knowledge alone that will be gained from this type of approach, especially when confined to the use of text. The use of open learning to support cognitive or perceptual skills may prove inadequate without the challenge and provocation that comes from face-to-face contact with other people. The bank manager who is given a series of open learning modules as a means of enhancing cognitive and perceptual skills will find 'open learning' a less than rewarding experience without further human support. Still on the subject of skill use, a case is recalled at a leading dental school of a dentist who injured people's jaws from time to time. This suggests that a motor skill was deficient in some way, however, the dentist continued to have a thriving practice and injured people came back for further treatment. The explanation given at the school was that the dentist compensated for the problem by having highly developed skills in personal relations, in other words, a sound combination of perceptual and cognitive skills.

Despite what theory can tell us about skill use, human beings will continue to defy expectation. At a training school for people with disabilities, a young man with two false arms performed gas welding, a task which a knowledge of skill use would suggest was impossible for him. The welder had two false arms and was able to make the necessary welding rod movements by a manipulation of his upper body. Two kinds of ability critical to the learning of welding are gross arm control and rate control and both were denied to this young man. The main lesson from this example is that people charged with analysing learning needs must keep an open mind at all times. While it may not be true that anyone, given the right support, can do anything, there is little harm and much potential benefit in believing that this is true and acting accordingly.

Types of ability

A problem that needs to be resolved before looking further at the relationship between ability and skill concerns the use of the word 'ability' when used simply as a label and when used as a concept. An example will illustrate the difference in use. If I say 'there is a wall', I am using the word 'wall' as a label to describe a pile of bricks held together with cement. However, if the wall happened to be that which once divided Germany then I may use the word 'boundary' or 'barrier' as a concept, depending upon how I conceptualize that same pile of bricks. The same is true of the word ability, when someone says a doctor has ability they are not making a distinction between effective or less effective ability, they are using the word as a label to describe the doctor and it automatically means good and positive. When we use the word ability as a concept the meaning is quite different.

When people have to transfer between jobs in a volatile labour market it is a combination of skill, knowledge and qualifications that is used to judge suitability for transfer. A skilled bank employee transferring to a post in marketing will assess which skills are to be retained and which skills need to be learned. It can be argued that *abilities* are more significant than skills when making such a transfer between jobs.

About forty abilities can be identified (Fleishman 1982). Thirty of these, which are felt to be most important in the learning of skills, are listed in an abilities exercise at the end of this chapter. At birth we have these thirty abilities and where some are either absent or impaired in some way we say a person has disabilities. However, it is rare for a person to have all abilities available at a high level of functioning; it is more normal for each of us to have certain abilities which can be called strong, some that are quite adequate and others that are weak. A person who has the abilities of inductive reasoning, word fluency and mathematical reasoning developed to a high level, tends to be described as intelligent, mainly because they ought to be good at doing intelligence tests. However, although the concept of intelligence is at times useful, it is a very limited way of looking at human behaviour, and in understanding how different people learn and the kind of support they may require it is of little value. If intelligence is to be used at all in this respect it is more useful to think of various types of intelligence or multiple intelligences. A person with highly developed abilities such as rate control, multi-limb coordination and visualization may, in bridging a river quickly with limited resources, behave far more intelligently than someone who is considered highly intelligent in terms of a test measurement. In general, a healthier approach to describing people when thinking of learning need is that we all have enormous potential in the abilities that are well developed and in the abilities that can be developed further.

Some abilities are difficult to develop and where these abilities are vital to the learning of a particular skill, training or any other means of learning support may prove to be unsuccessful. The abilities that appear to be resistant to development are colour discrimination, visualization, rate control, general hearing and originality. At least four of these abilities are vital to learning the skill of hairdressing at a high level of performance, which helps to explain why so few reach this level. It is what the person brings to the learning situation rather than the learning itself that largely determines success. For trainees who experience difficulty in breaking through to a higher level of performance, it is likely that their learning needs lie in the development of the critical abilities, if this is possible. The same four abilities are also very important to the learning of high level welding. One of the premier welding centres can sometimes record only six successes at this level from as many as two hundred trainees.

Wherever these particular abilities play a significant part in the learning of a skill, the task of selecting for trainability becomes as important as the learning support available. In contrast, other abilities can develop from being quite weak to being strong as a result of effective learning support. It is not uncommon for the abilities of number facility and mathematical reasoning to be weak after more than ten years of schooling but suddenly a different approach linked to more practical application of mathematics can result in skilled performance whenever these abilities are used. Certain abilities can be developed to compensate for weakness in others, as in the cases of the dentist and the young gas welder described in the previous section.

The linking of abilities to our learning of skills and knowledge will be explored later in the book using practical examples.

How abilities transfer between jobs

Most jobs require the use of skills that can be described as low-level, high-level or moderate-level. For each skill that we use there are normally from one to four abilities that help to explain both how we learn and how we eventually perform. From this knowledge we can say that a job that requires the use of four distinct skills will also require the use of certain abilities, let us say eight. If a person is performing this job to a high level of performance we can confidently say that the eight particular abilities are also functioning at a reasonably high level, unless, as noted in the previous section, one ability is compensating for a weakness in another. If this person transfers to another posting doing the same job then both skills and abilities also transfer. However, if this person decides to change jobs there are two questions to be asked about transfer: How many of the previous skills transfer? How many of the previous abilities transfer? Unfortunately, most transfers are made only on the basis of qualifications and skills. In other words if an alternative job does not share the same qualifications and skills requirement then transfer may well be thought impossible. It may be that two jobs do not have the same skill requirement but they do share the same abilities requirement.

An example of abilities transfer occurred during the movement from old print technology to new print technology when most of the traditional printing skills became obsolete. The belief of some printers that they could perform the job of sub-editor was thought unrealistic, because they were not graduates and some of the job skills were different. When an assessment of trainability demonstrated that abilities could transfer, the change between jobs was made successfully. In other words, if someone has demonstrated abilities in one job, then that person can transfer to another job that shares the same ability requirements even though the skills may be quite different. It can confidently be predicted that the person will quickly benefit from learning support and adapt to the new skills without too much difficulty.

Knowledge of the transfer of abilities is particularly relevant to the development of new working practices brought about through new technology. As explained earlier, skills today are increasingly of the cognitive and perceptual type and have shorter learning and practice periods. This allows for people to make two or more changes in jobs and skill use, and in fact conduct more than one job at the same time. Some abilities are more relevant to cognitive and perceptual skills than others, so there is an increased probability that jobs requiring these types of skill will have some abilities in common too. In many cases, transfer between jobs is easier than has been previously believed.

Knowledge use

People's knowledge also transfers along with skills and abilities. Knowledge is frequently tapped at various sources when performing cognitive and perceptual skills, and knowledge about how inanimate objects behave is frequently used during the practice of motor skills. A feature of technological development over the past twenty years has been easier access to knowledge; knowledge, like water, is now on tap. The pace of technological change is now so great that few people can expect to have all the knowledge they need, but they do require ready access to what is relevant and available. In identifying learning support the core knowledge requirement must be recognized and then people should learn how to access knowledge as they need it. The skilled nurse requires a sizeable core of knowledge to hand; a nurse who regularly consults manuals does not inspire confidence. However, nurses need regularly to up-date their knowledge, and learning support in the form of channels for information flow and ready access to sources of new information form an important part of the job.

Linking skills, knowledge and abilities

How we learn skills and knowledge is linked to the various abilities that enable us to carry out the learning. When deciding upon what needs to be learned we can concentrate upon knowledge only or upon skills only and this is how training needs analysis has been commonly performed. It is said that for any job there can exist a gap between existing skills and knowledge and desired skills and knowledge. Various methods have been used to help give an accurate measurement of this gap and to assess how far training can be expected to fill the gap. The fluid nature of employment means that we have to recognize a more complex relationship between skills, knowledge and abilities. There are at least nineteen events that can provide reasons for learning new skills and knowledge and at each event the influence of abilities plays a significant role. The common events are listed in Figure 2.3.

Each event involves a change of some kind which in turn can lead to a gap between present skills, knowledge and abilities. The strategy for analysing learning needs must also take account of which type of event is causing the need to learn; in most cases it will be one of those listed in Figure 2.3, but there may be other causes. The main reason for identifying the driving force behind the need to learn is that it may provide clues as to what needs to be learned.

A number of companies are now making moves towards more flexible working and 'flexible working' would be stated as the driving force for learning needs in this case. Working flexibly can be seen as a skilled activity in itself, in addition to any further skills that need to be learned. A person may be versatile in being able to perform a number of skilled activities but being flexible involves being able to switch readily between activities, a skill that uses abilities such as selective attention, time-sharing, information ordering and speed of focusing. The analysis of learning needs where new technology has been introduced can be problematic. One

---

- Promotion
- Sideways movement
- A new job
- Introduction of a new technology
- Introduction of a new method of working
- Introduction of a new process
- A move to multi-skilling
- A move to dual-skilling
- Introduction of flexible working
- Improvement of skills and/or knowledge
- Loss of market share
- Take-over
- Move to home-based working
- Move to part-time working
- Flattening of the organizational structure
- Move to a semi-automated process
- Reduction/expansion of staff numbers
- Move to employ older workers
- Re-allocation of responsibilities

Figure 2.3 Events that generate learning needs

problem is that meaningful questions cannot be asked because insufficient basic knowledge is available. To assess the gap to be filled in the requirements of a job you need a clear picture of where you are at present and where you want to be in the future. A group exercise using the technique of storyboard can indicate more clearly the kinds of skill and knowledge that will be involved.

Where promotion is the driving force, identification of learning need takes on a different requirement again. Here there can be a possibility that all skills of the previous position are transferred to the new appointment. This usually occurs when there is an unclear picture of what skilled performance ought to look like in the new position. The training needs of directors and senior managers are not particularly well served in the training literature. New directors and senior managers, like everyone new to a job, can expect to have learning needs. To emphasize this point, it should be recognized that the skills of the previous management appointment will not necessarily transfer and will at least need the addition of further skills.

Summary

It ought to be apparent from this description of skills, knowledge and abilities that a complex set of relationships exists between them. New work patterns, and those that can be predicted with any confidence, can use skills, knowledge and abilities in very different ways. Different emphasis is placed on certain skills or abilities and differences can be seen in the application of core knowledge in the assessment of non-core knowledge. Before any analysis of learning needs can be carried out effectively there must be some understanding of these differences. Primarily, it is people who are responsible for analysing needs who ought to have this clear understanding, but there is a case for making at least an appreciation of skills knowledge and abilities available to others. The abilities exercise in the next section can be used for this purpose.

Abilities exercise

Whenever we learn a skill the outcome is partly explained by how certain abilities are used, for example, learning to form clay into a piece of pottery requires the use of four or five separate abilities, depending upon how the skill is performed. The use of abilities applies to all the skills we learn. Unless physically impaired in some way we have, at birth, all the recognized abilities; thirty of these are listed in this exercise. If you have particular difficulty in learning a certain skill one cause of the difficulty is often that an ability required for that skill is, in your case, naturally weak or not well developed. In some cases more than one of the required abilities are weak or not well developed, and then there are serious difficulties in learning that skill.

An ability is said to be weak or strong, as the case may be, when it is extremely difficult, or impossible, to improve it through practice. Examples of such abilities are visualization, general hearing and colour discrimination. Abilities are said to be not well developed when for some reason you have not had the opportunity to practise their use. You may have abilities which are naturally highly developed, such as all the abilities required to be an oil painter, but if you do not have the opportunity to use this particular group of abilities by learning to paint the fact will go unnoticed.

The exercise that follows is in two parts. The first part is concerned with the level of your abilities, and the second part looks at the abilities required to perform a particular job, either your current job, one that you are thinking of doing, or any other job that is of interest to you.

Purpose of the exercise

The purpose of this exercise is to raise your awareness of the abilities that are used whenever a skill is learned, and of how these abilities influence the tasks and functions which we perform as part of a job. The benefits that can be gained from this exercise are listed below:

- To guide the transfer from one job to another. If the proposed job shares a similar ability profile to the previous job it can be confidently predicted that learning new skills and adapting to the new position will occur without too much difficulty.
- Where a proposed job is different in terms of the abilities profile, people can compare the proposed job with their own assessment of abilities and look for a significant match or mismatch to help guide decision-making.
- When trainers, teachers or tutors attempt to explain why someone has difficulty in learning a skill or grasping an idea, it is helpful to discuss the possibility that certain abilities are either weak or not well developed.
- When there is uncertainty about the type of career to follow it is helpful to compare the ability profile of individuals with the profiles of a range of jobs.
- To overturn the mistaken idea that such a quality as 'general intelligence' exists. People display different levels of so-called intelligence only in terms of specific situations; you may be 'highly intelligent' in some circumstances but not in others. So-called intelligence tests are not worth the paper they consume. We need to replace the idea of intelligence with an appreciation of our strengths and weaknesses in terms of how abilities are used in the work we do.
- When taking part in a multi-skill programme it is helpful to compare the various skills in terms of the abilities needed to learn them. Being able to perform one skill may mean that a person is more than 50 per cent towards learning another skill. Thus, instead of learning from scratch you can demonstrate that the person can already effectively perform some of the required abilities.

How to use the exercise

When you have completed both parts of the exercise a comparison can be made between them: is there a match or a mismatch? You can draw your own conclusions from this comparison.

A number of people employed in the same job can complete the second part of the exercise independently, and then compare their results. After some discussion they will be able to reach some agreement about the level of abilities needed. This information can be very helpful to people who are thinking of taking up this type of work.

One way to make a quick comparison is to join the crosses you have made on the first part of the exercise by drawing straight lines between them. You can then hold your sheet and one completed by someone else up to the light to see how closely the 'profile' made by the lines matches. Another way is to copy your results onto a transparency that has a photocopy of the sheet upon it. A comparison can then be made with other copied results by using an overhead projector.

If two jobs (A & B) share very similar ability requirements, then someone capable of performing job A should have confidence in learning and adapting to job B because it is essentially *abilities* that transfer when you change jobs, rather than *skills*.

Before completing the exercise do read the definition of abilities which follows.

Definition of the abilities

The abilities are listed alphabetically and, for example purposes only, each definition is followed by the titles of four jobs that would typically require use of the ability being described.

1. **Arm–hand steadiness**
    The ability to maintain steady controlled use of arm and hand, whether in a moving or static position.
    (welder, sign-writer, dentist, surgeon)
2. **Attention to detail**
    The ability to concentrate upon the smallest detail of a task so that nothing is left undone.
    (surgeon, aircraft maintenance technician, car mechanic, editor)
3. **Body orientation**
    The ability to judge where you are in relation to another person or an object, or where they are in relation to you.
    (footballer, lorry driver, diver, dancer)
4. **Colour discrimination**
    The ability to detect fine differences between colours, and to match colours.
    (painter, printer, electronic engineer, fashion designer)

5. **Deductive reasoning**
The ability to work from general rules and arrive at detailed logical answers or solutions.
(solicitor, tax inspector, surveyor, bank manager)

6. **Dynamic strength**
The ability to exert muscle force repeatedly or continuously over long periods; the resistance to muscle fatigue.
(vitreous china caster, coalminer, shipbuilding worker, road builder)

7. **Finger dexterity**
The ability to make skilled coordinated movement of the fingers of one or both hands.
(stringed instrument musician, jeweller, keyboard operator, fine art painter)

8. **Flexibility of focusing**
The ability to recognize quickly a known pattern or piece of information among a complex collection of patterns or information.
(proofreader, instrument panel controller, quality inspector, air disaster investigator)

9. **Flexibility of movement**
The ability to use whole-body movement in completing a task by bending, stretching, twisting or reaching.
(farrier, newspaper press minder, bricklayer, nurse)

10. **General hearing**
The ability to detect and discriminate among sounds which vary in pitch and/or loudness, and to locate the source of specific sounds.
(marine engineer, music conductor, machine troubleshooter, plumber)

11. **Idea fluency**
The ability to produce ideas, 'to think on your feet' and to see beyond a common fixed idea.
(production controller, quality circle member, project team member, planner)

12. **Inductive reasoning**
The ability to combine separate pieces of information to form general rules or conclusions; to think of reasons why particular factors go together.
(medical practitioner, accident examiner, engineering technician, police detective)

13. **Information ordering**
The ability to follow rules and instructions by arranging the relevant information in a sequence that can be followed reliably.
(process operator, operating theatre nurse, insurance salesperson, librarian)

14. **Manual dexterity**
The ability to make coordinated and skilled movements with arms and/or hands in such tasks as assembly and the use of tools.
(carpenter, glass-blower, welder, electronic assembler)

15. **Mathematical reasoning**
The ability to solve problems by using appropriate mathematical methods, and to understand mathematical concepts.
(engineering designer, systems analyst, statistician, research scientist)

16. **Memory**
The mental ability to recall words, numbers, graphics and sequences of operations.
(nurse, referee, airport check-in staff, actor)

17. **Multi-limb coordination**
The ability to coordinate the movement of more than one limb at the same time, for example, two arms and legs in driving.
(fork-lift truck operator, heavy-duty sewing machinist, car driver, potter)

18. **Number facility**
The ability to add, subtract, multiply, estimate, and use percentages accurately and quickly.
(bank personnel, accountant, commodity dealer, shop assistant)

19. **Originality**
The ability to think of unusual or novel ideas that can help provide creative solutions to problems, or help provide new products.
(clothes designer, project manager, window-dresser, management consultant)

20. **Perceptual speed**
The ability to make comparisons between letters, numbers, objects, and patterns quickly and accurately. The items may be grouped together, occur one after the other, or may involve making a comparison between presented items and items that have been remembered.
(printer, helicopter observer, power station operator, coin quality inspector)

21. **Problem sensitivity**
The ability to sense when something is wrong, or is likely to go wrong.
(aircraft pilot, machine operator, hairdresser, supervisor)

22. **Rate control**
The ability to judge speed and to adjust controls and/or limb movement in response to any change in speed.
(aircraft pilot, welder, packaging-machine operator, racing car driver)

23. **Selective attention**
The ability to concentrate upon a task without being distracted by events that are not part of the task.
(stockmarket dealer, electronic assembler, traffic police, referee)

24. **Speed of focusing**
The ability to organize different pieces of information into a recognizable pattern so that results can be described verbally, or can be acted upon in a practical way.
(air traffic controller, commodity dealer, radar observer, insurance claims analyst)

25. **Stamina**
The ability to perform physical tasks over prolonged periods of time while maintaining normal breathing and efficiency.
(oil-rig driller, farmer, chef, footballer)

26. **Static strength**
The ability to use muscle force to lift, push, pull or carry objects; the maximum force that someone can exert for a brief period of time.
(warehouse packer, nurse, building-site hod carrier, police officer)

27. **Time-sharing**
The ability to transfer quickly and efficiently between different types of information, and to switch attention.
(librarian, multi-skilled technician, police officer, nurse)

28. **Visual acuity**
The ability to see the finest detail possible with the naked eye when looking at an object.
(art dealer, picture restorer, electronic circuit inspector, surgeon)

29. **Visualization**
The ability to imagine what something will look like from the description given, and to imagine any changes in shape, position or state when these have been described to you, without actually seeing the object being described.
(mould-maker, hairdresser, instrument panel operator, designer)

30. **Word fluency**
The ability to make full use of words; to understand meaning and to be able to apply words appropriately in both report writing and in expressing ideas.
(journalists, member of parliament, professional engineer, teacher)

Completing the exercise

You are now ready to complete both parts of the exercise. Part 1 is entitled 'Abilities and you'; Part 2, 'Abilities and a job'. Refer back to the list of definitions of abilities as necessary.

The levels of abilities that you are asked to choose are explained below. Refer back to these explanations if in doubt.

Part 1:   Abilities and you

Highly developed:	You are confident that, in your case, there is little scope for improving upon the ability.
Adequate:	You can use the ability to satisfy any requirements where it is needed.
Underdeveloped:	You need to have the opportunity to improve the level of the ability.
Weak:	In your opinion it is not realistic to expect any improvement in your use of the ability.
Do not know:	You have not had the opportunity to use or think about the ability.

Part 2:   Abilities and a job

Very important:	The job could not be performed to the best possible standard without the use of the ability.
Necessary:	The ability is needed if at least one function is to be performed satisfactorily.
Useful:	The job can be performed without using the ability but at times it may enhance the completion of a task.
Not used:	The job does not require the use of the ability.
Do not know:	You cannot recognize use of the ability, but are not sure enough to say that it is not used.

Abilities exercise 1:   Abilities and you

Copy the page, and enter a cross in the appropriate box. Do this for *every* ability.

	Highly developed	Adequate	Under-developed	Weak	Do not know
1. Arm–hand steadiness	☐	☐	☐	☐	☐
2. Attention to detail	☐	☐	☐	☐	☐
3. Body orientation	☐	☐	☐	☐	☐
4. Colour discrimination	☐	☐	☐	☐	☐
5. Deductive reasoning	☐	☐	☐	☐	☐
6. Dynamic strength	☐	☐	☐	☐	☐
7. Finger dexterity	☐	☐	☐	☐	☐
8. Flexibility of focusing	☐	☐	☐	☐	☐
9. Flexibility of movement	☐	☐	☐	☐	☐
10. General hearing	☐	☐	☐	☐	☐
11. Idea fluency	☐	☐	☐	☐	☐
12. Inductive reasoning	☐	☐	☐	☐	☐
13. Information ordering	☐	☐	☐	☐	☐
14. Manual dexterity	☐	☐	☐	☐	☐
15. Mathematical reasoning	☐	☐	☐	☐	☐
16. Memory	☐	☐	☐	☐	☐
17. Multi-limb coordination	☐	☐	☐	☐	☐
18. Number facility	☐	☐	☐	☐	☐
19. Originality	☐	☐	☐	☐	☐

20.   Perceptual speed   ❏   ❏   ❏   ❏   ❏

21.   Problem sensitivity   ❏   ❏   ❏   ❏   ❏

22.   Rate control   ❏   ❏   ❏   ❏   ❏

23.   Selective attention   ❏   ❏   ❏   ❏   ❏

24.   Speed of focusing   ❏   ❏   ❏   ❏   ❏

25.   Stamina   ❏   ❏   ❏   ❏   ❏

26.   Static strength   ❏   ❏   ❏   ❏   ❏

27.   Time-sharing   ❏   ❏   ❏   ❏   ❏

28.   Visual acuity   ❏   ❏   ❏   ❏   ❏

29.   Visualization   ❏   ❏   ❏   ❏   ❏

30.   Word fluency   ❏   ❏   ❏   ❏   ❏

Abilities exercise 2:   Abilities and a job

Copy the page, and enter a cross in the appropriate box. Do this for *every* ability.

	Very important	Necessary	Useful	Not used	Do not know
1. Arm–hand steadiness	☐	☐	☐	☐	☐
2. Attention to detail	☐	☐	☐	☐	☐
3. Body orientation	☐	☐	☐	☐	☐
4. Colour discrimination	☐	☐	☐	☐	☐
5. Deductive reasoning	☐	☐	☐	☐	☐
6. Dynamic strength	☐	☐	☐	☐	☐
7. Finger dexterity	☐	☐	☐	☐	☐
8. Flexibility of focusing	☐	☐	☐	☐	☐
9. Flexibility of movement	☐	☐	☐	☐	☐
10. General hearing	☐	☐	☐	☐	☐
11. Idea fluency	☐	☐	☐	☐	☐
12. Inductive reasoning	☐	☐	☐	☐	☐
13. Information ordering	☐	☐	☐	☐	☐
14. Manual dexterity	☐	☐	☐	☐	☐
15. Mathematical reasoning	☐	☐	☐	☐	☐
16. Memory	☐	☐	☐	☐	☐
17. Multi-limb coordination	☐	☐	☐	☐	☐
18. Number facility	☐	☐	☐	☐	☐
19. Originality	☐	☐	☐	☐	☐

20.	Perceptual speed	❏	❏	❏	❏	❏
21.	Problem sensitivity	❏	❏	❏	❏	❏
22.	Rate control	❏	❏	❏	❏	❏
23.	Selective attention	❏	❏	❏	❏	❏
24.	Speed of focusing	❏	❏	❏	❏	❏
25.	Stamina	❏	❏	❏	❏	❏
26.	Static strength	❏	❏	❏	❏	❏
27.	Time-sharing	❏	❏	❏	❏	❏
28.	Visual acuity	❏	❏	❏	❏	❏
29.	Visualization	❏	❏	❏	❏	❏
30.	Word fluency	❏	❏	❏	❏	❏

3 Developing a strategy

Self-diagnosis

What do the terms 'strategy' and 'strategic thinking' mean to you? Think for a moment about a strategy for analysing learning needs and support. What would be included in such a strategy? Is there a series of steps or phases to be worked through, either as part of a continuous process at work or as a one-off identification exercise? What part does planning play in this strategy? What techniques could be included, if any? Will one strategy serve all the learning needs analysis you are likely to encounter? When you have answered these questions, and have thought about what a strategy is composed of, continue with this section.

When developing a strategy for analysing learning needs two types of technique can be applied: information gathering techniques and analysis techniques. To discover which type of technique you are using check on the final or likely output from the technique's application. If the output is simply a pile of information about a subject then you have been using an information gathering technique. If the information is divided into separate piles or categories with various types of comparison made between them such as correlations, relationships, strengths, weaknesses or feasibility, then you have been using an analysis technique.

Figure 3.1 below is in the form of an exercise. Simply photocopy the page or use a separate sheet of paper with columns and headings drawn, then indicate your level of familiarity with each technique by ticking the appropriate column.

Technique	Have used	Known	Not known
Listening and questioning	......	....	....
Critical incident technique	....	....	....
Brainstorming/Brainwriting	....	....	....
Survey questionnaire	....	....	....
Force field analysis	....	....	....
Abilities approach	....	....	....
AET	....	....	....
Protocol analysis	....	....	....
Repertory grid	....	....	....
Skills analysis	....	....	....
SWOT	....	....	....
Delphi	....	....	....
Nominal group	....	....	....
Cartoon storyboard	....	....	....

Figure 3.1   Strategy techniques exercise

As a result of completing this exercise, you may recognize that you have already sufficient familiarity to cover both information gathering and analysis. Or, you may feel that more work is required in gaining skill in the use of certain techniques.

Developing a strategy

An important aspect of strategy use is that it helps you to respond to changing circumstances. Built into any effective and reliable strategy is the means to ask 'What if?' and 'What now?' questions. It helps to have a toolbox of techniques that can be called upon and the choice of technique(s) is determined by the particular circumstances. Techniques can help us anticipate events and plan for our needs; at other times they can help us react quickly to events or when knowledge of needs becomes urgent.

There is an important distinction between anticipating needs in the near future and needs for the longer term. If a need is for the longer foreseeable future then support will be looked for in education. If the need is job-specific and required very soon or in the near future then support may well be found in training. As explained in the previous chapter, it is difficult, if not impossible, to train for the long-term future and this holds true when applied to a nation as well as to individual companies. Training must be job-specific and reinforced immediately by practice on that job if it is to be valid and worthwhile. A few motor skills like bicycle riding or shoelace tying can be stockpiled for future use without extensive practice, but most other motor skills and nearly all perceptual and cognitive skills are lost over time unless there is extensive post-learning practice; even then skills can seriously deteriorate. Thus awareness of timing is an important part of developing a strategy.

A framework for a strategy is shown in Figure 3.2. This is a guide only, as you will eventually find that you adopt favourite techniques and timing will be determined and a sequence of tasks developed that is appropriate to your requirements.

In Figure 3.2, the 'trigger' for an analysis of learning needs comes from two broad areas. One is based upon current events that are either planned or enforced by circumstances, (unplanned) and the other is based upon an analysis of business planning.

Figure 2.3 (p.23) shows that a number of events such as the introduction of a new process, a new technology or a take-over could typically spring from business plan information. Other events such as promotions, or a move to semi-automated processes could be part of planning that is current and continuous; on the other hand a loss of market share or a sudden take-over can generate learning needs from enforced circumstances. This leads to the next step in the strategic framework: setting the time-scale. Apart from enforced circumstances, the occurrence of all other events should be known sufficiently in advance to allow for thorough information gathering and analysis, including consultation with people who are going to be influenced most. Even in the case of enforced events time should be allowed for consultation about learning needs, but in reality the most that can be expected is a 'quick and dirty' run through of information gathering and analysis.

Once you have analysed learning needs and support, it is important to give feedback to the people involved, and also to the initial source of the need. At this stage you are checking that people's concerns have been taken into account in providing support. In returning to current initiatives or the business plan you can check that no requisite skills, knowledge and abilities have been overlooked.

In strategy development it is important to avoid the problem-trap, that is, the tendency of some people to call nearly all tasks 'problems'. This may

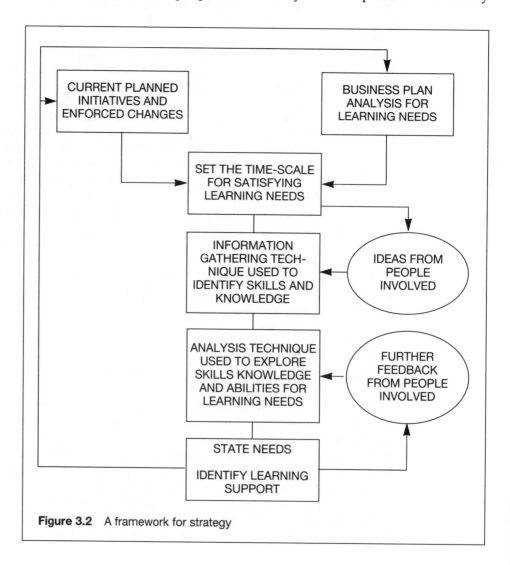

Figure 3.2   A framework for strategy

be a result of an over-emphasis on problem-solving in schools, or of the use of packaged problem-solving methods. Unfortunately it leads to a burdensome view of life and is not to be recommended. Chambers Dictionary defines a problem as 'a matter difficult to settle or solve, a source of perplexity'. The analysis of needs, of whatever kind, should be viewed as a challenge or as an interesting or even exciting task – not as a problem. Although at some stage a genuine problem may arise, such as discovering a gap between the need you have identified and the means of providing an acceptable support.

Think about the extent to which your own work is problem-driven and whether there is a tendency to view tasks, such as deciding upon training methods, as a problem instead of a challenge.

Summary

A strategy for analysing learning needs must contain, at least, the following elements:

- An awareness of broader issues, both within the organization and beyond the boundary of the organization, that will enable you to anticipate possible needs long before they become an urgent necessity.
- A 'toolbox' of techniques that you have practised and feel comfortable in using, which are also acceptable to those who will be involved in the task of analysis.
- An agreed sequence and pattern of activities that can take you from initial awareness or 'sensing' of a possible learning need to a solution. The solution should be a description of the need (or no need) plus a description of the appropriate means of support where necessary.
- A description of the type of skill, knowledge and appropriate abilities where any need is said to exist.
- A knowledge of the time-scale involved, so that you can decide whether the support needed is more likely to be education, training, self-guided learning or mentoring.
- An attitude towards the analysis of learning need that enables you to regard it as a challenge rather than a problem.

4　Gathering the information

The aim of this chapter is to describe in more detail the techniques that can be used for gathering information about a job or a series of tasks in terms of the skills, knowledge and abilities necessary for effective performance.

Listening and questioning

The two skills of listening and questioning are combined here to be used as a technique. General hearing is an ability; you are born either able to hear or unable to hear and this ability is unlikely to improve over time unless some artificial aid is used. Listening, in contrast, is a skill that we have learned to exercise either very well, very badly or somewhere in between. Of all our activities involving the use of words, listening takes up the highest proportion of our time at 45 per cent. This compares with writing, talking and reading that account for the remaining 55 per cent. As a skill, listening can be improved with learning and practice. Questioning too can be improved. Although word fluency is an ability, putting together words into the form of questions is a skill, and questioning can be performed very well or very badly.

Given that listening and questioning are so important to our general well-being, it is difficult to understand why these skills are not recognized as a source of learning needs in our schools. The skills are seldom taught except in customer relations programmes and in the training of air traffic controllers. In the United States of America greater emphasis is put upon these skills – when an American is introduced to someone and fails to grasp the name, he or she will quickly check it to ensure that listening has been effective. This is not a common response among people elsewhere. Listening in this way is known as 'active listening', because people who practise it can be seen to be listening and they treat it as an activity.

One of the strongest aids to the improvement of our listening and questioning skills is the appreciation that they are skills and that, like any other skill, they can be greatly improved through learning and practice. In order to understand more about listening and questioning and how to improve their use as a technique, we will first discuss them separately and then look at the two together.

Listening

Probably the most important factor to be aware of when setting out to improve listening is that the skill can be used highly selectively: we hear what we want to hear.

Here is an exercise that you may like to try. Sit with a friend in a busy shopping centre, about three feet apart, and do not speak for five minutes. During this time each of you make notes about what you can hear and when the five minutes is up compare your results. There is every probability that some differences will exist despite the fact that you were exposed to the same sounds and voices. Some of the differences may be explained by the level of general hearing ability, such as in picking up distant or faint sounds, but other differences will be due to our selective listening. This observation applies equally to listening for the purpose of collecting learning needs information. It is also relevant to some of the jobs that may be investigated, such as nursing, police work, welding or machine operation; all require the skill of listening and there may be potential for improving that skill through learning.

Another important aspect of listening is the outward signs that we give to the person or people being listened to; this is called non-verbal behaviour. If you appear from your approach to be someone who listens, there is a greater chance of obtaining the information you seek. So, what are the typical non-verbal behaviours that mark you out as a good listener? The first to note is your reaction on being introduced to someone. Do you react like the typical American described above and check if you did not quite catch the name, or do you let the mis-hearing pass and avoid use of that person's name, hoping to find it out later? If you check whenever a word or comment is not clear you will seem to be listening, even if your hearing is not too strong!

Another non-verbal behaviour to note is standing or sitting in a relaxed way. People who sit with arms folded across the chest, or with clenched fists, or with their knees tightly pressed together will often appear defensive and unwilling to participate fully. The most likely outcome of such an unrelaxed stance is that information will not flow easily towards you despite the questioning. If your stance is relaxed, with arms and palms open, the clear signs are that you wish to listen and hear all that is said.

Another useful method in gathering information is to use silence. It is not uncommon in discussion, especially in business meetings, for people to feel that every available second must be filled with the spoken word. The active listener is happy to spend between ten and fifteen seconds in complete silence. This may sound like a very short time, but in the middle of discussion it seems a very long time; try it. A likely result of speaking when less than five seconds of silence have passed is to lose some information that could have been very useful because you have interrupted a thought process.

Eye contact is also important to active listening. The ideal amount of contact seems to be around 30 per cent of any one chunk of discussion. From experience you will know the feeling that comes from having someone listen to you without maintaining sufficient eye contact. Maintaining eye contact for less than 10 per cent of time is disconcerting and 20 per cent is around the minimum for effective active listening. With little eye contact you may be listening extremely well, but you will *appear* to be not listening and the other person will lose interest. On the other hand eye contact can be overdone. From experience you will know the uncomfortable effect of having more than 70 per cent eye contact; 50 per cent of spoken time appears to be an acceptable maximum.

How close one person stands to another when listening can be significant, particularly for investigators who have to gather information from people of another culture. The person questioning and listening should establish an acceptable distance and not make the other person adjust position. It is for this reason that appropriate use of non-verbal behaviour can be recognised as a learning need for people new to working in foreign countries.

Whenever possible avoid the barrier of desk or counter when gathering information. The active listener normally tries to arrange for the approach to be similar to that of two friends meeting.

Some people prefer to listen in silence and if this applies to you it is necessary to make full use of the effective non-verbal behaviours outlined above. There are verbal behaviours, too, that help us demonstrate active listening. These consist of words and sounds. The words are familiar, such as well!, right!, I see, okay, true!, never! and so on. The sounds include, mm, mm-mm, phew, cough, and so on. All such words and sounds help to promote active listening. Another way to use verbal behaviour is to make a habit of quickly summarizing what has been said. This is especially helpful when collecting information about learning needs.

The main points about active listening are summarized in Figure 4.1. Check to see how closely you follow these behaviours.

Questioning

The non-verbal behaviours important to active listening apply also to the skill of questioning. A relaxed stance is especially important because the act

- Be aware of how selective your listening can be.
- Allow silence of up to fifteen seconds at any one time.
- Maintain relaxed limb and body posture.
- Use facial expressions to show attention.
- Check every word or comment that is misheard or unclear.
- Maintain eye contact, ideally for a third of listening time but not more than half.
- Summarize what you understand the speaker to have said.
- Avoid material barriers of any kind.

Figure 4.1 Active listening behaviours

of questioning can be threatening to the other person. A typical reaction to being questioned is to wonder 'Why is this person really asking me these questions?' The significant word is 'really' because so often people think that there is a hidden agenda behind the questions. A golden rule in the use of questioning is never to launch straight into the task of information gathering. The initial contact has to be as open as possible. The best way to achieve this is to begin by changing roles: invite the other person to ask *you* questions. Certainly there is risk in doing this, but unless you can satisfy any doubts the other person may have then you have no valid reason for continuing the questioning. Both parties must be comfortable with the situation and this applies equally to gathering information from a group of people.

There are two broad categories of questioning: affective questioning seeks to gather information about beliefs, values, interests and attitudes; detailed questioning places emphasis upon so-called facts that include quantity, direction, control and timing. Although the two categories are often used in tandem, it is helpful to keep them separate when learning how to improve questioning.

An extreme example of the use of affective questioning would be to seek learning needs from a session of counselling. An extreme example of detailed questioning would involve seeking learning needs in a chemical plant.

Questions are most commonly thought of as being either open or closed: open questions allow respondents a free rein; closed questions can be answered by only 'yes' or 'no'. Closed questions begin with the words 'is', 'will', 'may' or 'were' and open questions are best started with the four 'Ws' of 'who', 'when', 'where' and 'what', with the word 'how' also being very useful. 'Why' questions should be treated with caution during learning needs analysis. Pat answers to why things happen the way they do are likely to be given. We need to discover causes of happenings and this normally requires both information gathering and analysis techniques. One very useful method of gathering information in an open way is to use a phrase that is not a question; say simply, 'Tell me about ...'.

A third general type of question is called semi-closed, for example asking 'How many times has this happened today?' The question begins in an open way but closes down to some specifics. To ask 'How many ways does this happen?' would be a very open alternative.

There are many other types of question apart from those discussed so far and knowledge about those that are important to the task of needs analysis helps us become more sensitive questioners. The types of question are listed below with examples:

- **What-if** questions are used to speculate about the likely outcomes of any change to working practices, e.g. 'Tell me, what do you think would happen if the supervisors were responsible for costing this process?'
- **Mirror** questions are used to reflect upon what has been said and help to clarify ideas. They can also be effective in prompting further ideas, e.g. 'You say there is too much to learn as a result of the change?'
- **Value** questions are used to gather attitudes, beliefs and particular interests, e.g. 'Tell me, where do you feel that a lack of skill really shows?'
- **Silence** is used when you infer that the respondent needs time to think; allowing silence is effectively asking another question.
- **Self-disclosure** questions are used when you wish to make your immediate thoughts known to the respondent. This can also prompt further ideas, e.g. 'It seems to me that training will do little to improve this situation, what do you think?'
- **Critical** questions are used when it is necessary to focus specifically upon a skilled behaviour, e.g. 'Initiative is used you say, will you describe an incident where initiative is used?' This form of question is part of the critical incident technique.
- **Summary** is used to pull information together and to clarify, e.g. 'Now as I understand it there are … Have you anything to add that could improve my understanding of this process?'

These seven types of question are open, with the exception of the first two, which are semi-closed. This ratio of 5:2 between open and semi-closed questions is one for which it is reasonable to aim. This does not mean that closed questions should never be used; there are occasions when such questions are of real value such as, 'Were you doing between 95 and 110 miles per hour down this road?' 'No Ocifer!' The main point is to use closed questions sparingly.

The technique of listening and questioning is fully developed when, like a foreign correspondent, you feel comfortable about going into any situation to ask questions and to practise active listening and as a result you overlook very little that could be of importance. Although the two skills go hand-in-glove there is value in concentrating first upon your listening skill, then upon your questioning skill, before putting the two together to form a well-honed information gathering technique.

Some very good text books have been written on this subject; some are specific to listening, to questioning, or to both (MacKay 1980, 1984, 1989), (Burley-Allen 1982) and (Steil 1983).

The critical incident technique

The critical incident technique (CIT) was developed during the Second World War in the USA by psychologist John Flanagan. The results of his work were published in a professional journal (Flanagan 1954), and this paper remains the only true guide to the subject. One of the main reasons for developing the technique was to help in the investigation of bombing raids over Germany. The aim was to discover the reasons for incidents of failure and because the skilled behaviour of the flight crews was one of the main variables in the investigation, one of the expected outputs was an analysis of learning needs.

Possibly the strongest claim to be made for the technique is that it is one of the most effective ways that people can be helped to articulate what it is they do when performing a skilled task. Occasionally an investigator will come across someone who can describe in great detail the behaviours that contribute towards skilled or unskilled performance. The example comes to mind of a 'top' hairdresser who talked through an expensive styling job while he performed it. The hairdresser was able to articulate the skill in such a way that key points emerged that had been ignored by hairdressers spoken to earlier. Other hairdressers talked about the skill of cutting but did not, like this hairdresser, point out that all the skill was in the non-cutting hand.

Another vital factor overlooked by other hairdressers concerned the ability of visualization. The highly skilled hairdresser is able to visualize a style and a mapping of the head in tandem and works towards the outcome. At present there is no known way to improve the ability of visu-alization; in some people it is strong and in others it is very weak. Such observations have significant implications for learning needs analysis. We might conclude, for example, that in order to rise above the basic high-street level of hairdressing it is necessary to have, among other abilities, strong visualization.

By using the critical incident technique with other hairdressers it was possible to approach the level of detail provided by the 'rare' individual. An important principle underlying the use of critical incidents is that jobs tend to contain 'padding', that is, tasks and skill use that do not contribute significantly to performance. On the other hand there are tasks and skill use that are critical to performance and the aim of the technique is to explore these incidents.

Within each incident, motor, perceptual or cognitive type skills can be identified. The technique is highly process-oriented. It is more concerned with how skilled behaviour can be described than with a product-oriented or outcome description, as in the case of competency statements. The process approach is vital to learning needs analysis; the knowledge gained from a product approach that someone can or cannot do a particular task is of little value to needs analysis. In most jobs understanding is important, but because it is difficult to assess it tends to be ignored in competency-based work; the needs associated with understanding cannot be ignored.

The critical incident technique can be used in three ways:

1.   Face-to-face interviewing.
2.   Group interview.
3.   Survey questionnaire.

The first two ways are preferable for detailed information gathering, while the questionnaire can be useful in targeting a larger population, although some essential detail is usually lost. A good plan, if resources allow, is to follow up the face-to-face work with a questionnaire.

The face-to-face interview begins with the investigator setting the scene, for example with a hospital surgeon. The first requirement is to specify the exact area of skill, knowledge and understanding to be explored. In this case it could be operation preparation, instrument selection, instrument use, entry procedures, manipulations, removal and/or placement of organs. It is also possible to agree this area prior to the actual critical incident contact. When the investigator and the surgeon are comfortable with the chosen area the more detailed investigation can begin.

When using the technique, the investigator asks very few questions, the skill lies in how prompts are used to help the respondent think through the various behaviours. However, some open and semi-closed questions are used to pump-prime the session. For example:

'Let us begin by looking at the use of a particular instrument. Which instrument would you say demanded the most skilled behaviour?'

This semi-closed question is being used to highlight the principle of critical incident use discussed earlier. In nearly all jobs there is a task which if performed well means that a person can be confidently expected to do all other tasks well. In a job as complex as that of a surgeon we are applying the principle to the task of using instruments. If someone can learn and perform to a skilled standard with one particular instrument then use of other instruments will confidently follow. Incidentally, when planning learning support it can be worthwhile to examine the most difficult task first. This is contrary to the idea of part-learning where there is a steady build up to the most difficult task; this issue will be discussed in more detail later.

When an instrument has been chosen the critical incident questioning can continue:

'What, more than anything, makes the difference between skilled and less skilled use of the instrument?'

The reply to such a question is normally in the form of an example or 'incident'. However, some less articulate people may simply reply with only three or four words, for example, 'It's all about confidence'.

'Fine, can you give me an example of what happens that makes you say it is about confidence?'

Whenever respondents have difficulty in articulating behaviours they can be helped by this type of probing. A common remark is for people to say something like, 'the operator needs to use initiative here'. In terms of analysing learning needs the word 'initiative' is of little value; there is not much you can do about initiative despite the claims of some outdoor education professionals to the contrary. What is needed is a description of a typical incident that makes the respondent use the word 'initiative', so the investigator follows with,

> 'What incident can you tell me about that makes you say that the operator needs to use initiative here?'

The reply now ought to be in the form of an incident, and should point to behaviour that is vital to the task being investigated. What often happens is that halfway through the description the respondent says, 'Wait a minute it's not really initiative I'm talking about is it?' Or, 'Now I come to think about it, if the process were better organized the operator would not need to use initiative'. This is fairly typical of work which calls for so-called initiative; the critical incident approach allows people to look with fresh eyes on a familiar, and at times a too-familiar situation.

To return to the surgeon, whenever the description of an incident is at an end, remember to use silence to make sure the surgeon has finished. Certain key words relevant to skill, knowledge or understanding can be picked up as prompts rather than as direct questions, for example, 'You mentioned angle three times'. Such a prompt should be sufficient to bring further detail about this aspect of instrument use. Other key words or phrases, such as 'sideways pressure?' or 'You say it is sensitive touch?' are explored in the same way by using only prompts. By now the investigator has notes about the first important aspect of using this particular instrument and other incidents that followed from the prompting. It would not be surprising to have five or six such incidents.

The next step is to say, 'What other incident can you give me that is important here?' The investigator *never* says, 'Are there any more incidents?' This is an invitation to opt out of the session. The investigator must be positive and probing to the end and it is the respondent who offers the suggestion that the topic is exhausted. The next and following incidents follow the same pattern of exploration, one or two questions, active listening, then probing, silence, then more probing until saturation is reached.

Saturation is of interest to anyone who wishes to explore in detail the use of skills in a job and the subsequent learning that may be needed. Saturation can be demonstrated very well through the use of critical incidents. An unwritten law about the number of people needed to saturate all that can be discovered about a skilled task, or group of tasks, which make up a job is that when six people have given contributions in the form of incidents, for about one hour each, the next person is unlikely to contribute anything further of any significance. One other person can then be seen to confirm that nothing has been missed. The next step is to give the total information to others who know the job and ask if anything is missing; it is seldom that anything further can be added.

For some jobs the point of saturation can be reached with less than six people but six is the normal maximum at which saturation is achieved. In the case of a particular task, as opposed to a whole job, the point of saturation is most often reached by seeing two people but a third is normally seen for confirmation purposes. Non-verbal behaviour is important when using this technique; although the investigator on seeing the sixth person will have listened to most of the incidents, the information must appear to be new and fresh to the investigator.

In the hospital case, when the full description of skill use has been gathered about the one particularly demanding instrument it is then possible to explore characteristics of the other instruments where they differ from this description. As a result of this critical incident exercise a comprehensive set of data will be available upon which to assess learning needs in the task of operating instrument use.

Information of this kind can also be used to design a simulated exercise around the most demanding aspects of the skilled behaviour. If someone is then taught to perform the simulated task and asked to do it unaided (allowing for any safety considerations), the outcome can be a good predictor of that person's potential to learn the skills – in other words, trainability. This is the basis of trainability testing (Craig 1985), in which a diagnostic test as opposed to a test which simply gives a pass or fail is used in the selection of people for jobs. When someone has completed a test of this kind, particular areas of weakness can be identified which then indicate possible learning needs. The same method has been used recently to select existing employees for programmes of training in new technology. Trainability testing is more face-valid, more content-valid and more reliable than the use of psychometric testing. The disadvantage is that trainability tests normally have to be customized, rather than bought 'off a shelf', and this makes the method costly. The cost–benefit analysis of this form of testing has to be established by the organization against its own particular requirements. Trainability is closely related to critical incident use and adds another dimension to the technique.

The critical incident technique has been used in over seven hundred reported investigations (Fivars 1980), having particular application for accident or failure investigation and for understanding the elements of skilled behaviour. In the case of accidents or failures, the technique can reveal incidents where the need for learning was a contributory factor and such information can form the basis for the design of subsequent learning support.

Brainstorming and brainwriting

Brainstorming, or what has become known as classic brainstorming, was developed by Osborn (Osborn 1963) and is one of the better known techniques. Sometimes it is used for problem-solving but as designed it cannot fulfil this function. The outcome of a brainstorming session is, or ought to be, a mass of ideas prompted by the question, 'How many ways can we think of for …?' The topics can be endless but our concern is about issues surrounding the use of skills, knowledge and understanding. Completing the question with the words '… increasing knowledge about our clients' needs' may well reveal one or more learning needs. Brainwriting provides a more anonymous way of conducting effectively the same exercise.

There are four basic rules to be observed when running a brainstorming session:

1. No fixed time limit, do not say, 'We will have a ten minute brainstorming session'.
2. All contributions are to be accepted without question.
3. There must be a facilitator who acts to encourage offers of ideas but never questions or changes what has been said.
4. No outside interruptions are allowed.

Between six and twelve people is the ideal size for a brainstorming group; fewer or more than this number begins to weaken the effect of the technique. It is quite possible for ten people to generate over two hundred ideas prompted by the one question. The facilitator should never say, 'Are there any more ideas' because this closes down the thought process. The approach has to be positive; there has to be a demand for ideas. Again, silence plays an important role. The facilitator must be happy to allow silence while the group members are thinking. The facilitator writes accurately the ideas upon a board or flip chart so that the group can view all ideas simultaneously. This is vital because the general picture that is building up can help trigger more ideas.

When saturation point has been reached the ideas are categorized into three types: good ideas, poor ideas and weirdo ideas. Dealing with each idea in turn the facilitator asks the group to allocate ideas to one of these categories. Interestingly, it is among the weirdo ideas that the occasional truly creative idea is to be found. At this point the technique can be extended to one of analysis by asking sub-groups of people to compare the ideas within each category and then come together to share their general conclusions from the exercise. The end result is normally a host of ideas, some insight, and information to aid further discussion.

Brainwriting as the name implies involves putting ideas down on paper. There are around seven or eight variations on this technique (Van Gundy 1988), but three are particularly appropriate to needs analysis. First, in the most basic method you sit down and record ideas from a private brainstorm. The second variation involves collecting ideas from people who have recorded them independently, but the people are not involved further. The third and possibly the most valuable variation is to collect written ideas independently and share them among the group; this is an essential part of the delphi technique which is described in the next chapter. Each of these approaches overcomes the problem that can be encountered in classic brainstorming of some people being intimidated by others and, as a result, becoming reluctant to participate.

Survey questionnaire

The survey questionnaire is possibly the most used and most abused method of gathering information. The technique needs to be used, if at all, with great caution when collecting information about learning needs. The pre-judgement of outcome is the principal disadvantage of using survey questionnaires. If you do not have an answer, you do not have a question, therefore to ask any question you need to have some idea about a possible answer; think about it. When people design questionnaires, the questions reflect the concerns of the designer more than the concerns of those who are asked to respond. When collecting information about skills, knowledge and ability requirements for the purpose of identifying learning needs, it is the concerns of people directly involved that should be reflected.

The pre-judgement problem can be overcome, but this is quite costly in terms of time and use of personnel. Probably the most effective method is to conduct face-to-face interviews of the critical incident type, with up to seven people, or until saturation is reached. The survey questions can then be based upon the principal concerns expressed through this in-depth investigation.

Another approach, to help avoid pre-judgement, is to design a questionnaire that contains mainly open questions, so that you gather spontaneous views about needs. Unfortunately, the interpretation and analysis of such questionnaires is time consuming and careful costing is recommended before use.

Important points to note in the wording of questions for needs analysis are listed below (for more detailed description of question wording and general questionnaire design, two excellent books are Labaw (1980) and Reeves (1981)):

- Never ask two questions in the space of one.
- Never make the answer to one question dependent upon the answer to an earlier question.
- Never ask questions that the survey population may not be able to answer.
- Never use wording beyond the reading age of the target population.
- Never become involved in and/or type questions.
- Never extend questions beyond two lines across an A4 sheet.
- Never ask 'why' questions.

Finally, the most important point to note about the use of a survey for analysing learning needs concerns feedback. Never attempt to use a questionnaire of this kind without having the means to give everyone who has been involved full feedback about the outcome.

Summary

Most of the techniques outlined in this chapter are quite well known and have been described as they apply to the analysis of learning needs. In the case of the critical incident technique, where there is much less available guidance, rather more detail has been provided. Part of developing a strategy for the analysis of needs is to think of information gathering on the one hand and analysis of the information on the other. The general idea is that you should develop and practise one or two appropriate techniques for gathering and for analysis. Guidance in the choice of techniques, by allowing for particular circumstances, will be covered later in the book when practical applications of the techniques are described.

5   Analysing the information

Once the phase of information gathering is complete, analysis is required of the various forms that information can take, that is, description, quantities, attitudes or frequencies. Analysis simply means breaking down information into appropriate parts so that meaningful comparisons can be made. There are many techniques of analysis but those described here relate to the analysis of learning needs. The first technique to be described provides a useful entry point into learning needs analysis. Then a very broad technique of job analysis will be discussed before moving into more detailed exploration of techniques that can be used for particular purposes. It is the selection, sequencing, application and interpretation of techniques that will provide you with the central structure of a learning needs analysis strategy.

The force field technique

The technique of force field was developed initially by Kurt Lewin (Majaro 1988), and provides a simple but effective approach to the initial identification of potential learning needs. The technique is used primarily where a change of some kind is taking place. A change in technology, a change in working practice or a change in company ownership can all lead to learning needs. A common aspect of change is the conflict between those forces that are driving, or 'for', the change and those that are restraining, or 'against', the change.

Inspection of typical force field diagrams (see Figure 5.1) show that driving forces are usually organization-based, and restraining forces come from the concerns of individuals. This observation leads in turn to the assumption that any learning needs to be derived from the driving forces will be those of the organization and those from the restraining forces will be related to the individuals involved. While certain exceptions do exist to this split between forces and the respective types of learning need, in general the assumption is valid. One of the themes of this book is that no real distinction ought to be made between learning needs of the organization and the learning needs of individuals. If an organization is not struc-

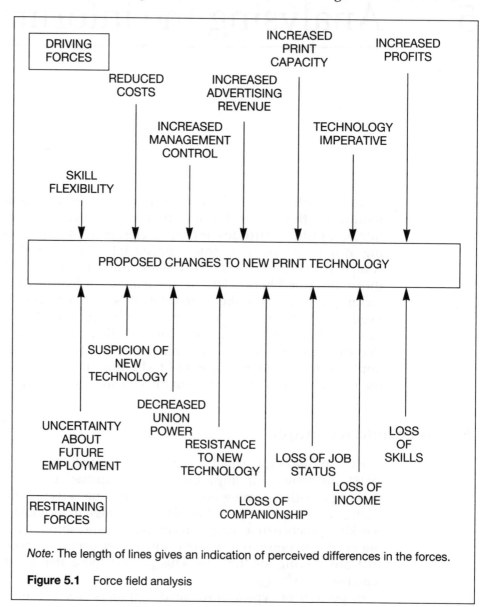

Note: The length of lines gives an indication of perceived differences in the forces.

Figure 5.1   Force field analysis

tured to operate in a way that encourages and allows individuals to learn, then the organization itself will not learn.

Part of Lewin's theory is the idea that initiatives can be taken that either have the effect of reducing the restraining forces or of increasing the driving forces as a means of facilitating the change. A key question to ask is, 'What type of learning can contribute most to achieving either reductions in restraining forces, increases in driving forces, or if possible, both?' In most cases of change there are a number of initiatives other than learning that can be considered. You need to be aware of these other initiatives so that learning needs can be put into a proper perspective. It may be that if certain initiatives are adopted there will be little need for learning support. On the other hand, a chosen initiative may itself demand some form of learning. In contrast the required initiative may be one that is best provided through a training programme.

Force field as a technique for needs analysis works best when combined with a delphi-type approach. (The full delphi technique is discussed in the next section.) Imagine the setting suggested by the change illustrated in Figure 5.1. A one-page brief description of the force field technique is sent to a number of people who are involved in the proposed change, ideally around fifteen. If this number is unrealistic, target as many people as possible, but hopefully more than two or three people. The description needs to contain a sample force field diagram on another subject, simply to provide an example. Each person is asked to produce their own diagram of the respective forces that they feel are critical to the proposed change. This exercise is completed independently. The investigator acts as facilitator and collects the diagrams before sending a complete set to each person with a proposed 'master' force field that has been derived from all of them. Each person can then offer any new ideas which are triggered by seeing the combined result and after some discussion a master diagram can be produced.

The initiatives that are identified through such an exercise may contain learning needs around skills (additional or improved), knowledge (actual or having access to the source) or understanding (awareness or at a deeper level).

Important points to note in the formulation of a force field are that the central horizontal box should contain a clear concise statement of the proposed change and the lines of force should be drawn so as to indicate differences in strength as you perceive them. This can be shown, either by varying the length of lines or by varying their thickness: the longer/thicker the line, the stronger the force. A short note is always needed to indicate how the force strengths have been shown. Also make it clear which forces are driving and which are restraining. The difference is not always obvious because whether a force is one or the other depends upon a person's point of view. Profit making may be stated as a driving force but someone with a different perception may view this as a restraining force, that is, they do not wish to produce profit or surplus value. Such differences are normally resolved in the delphi-type exercise and serve to clarify the view of any change to processes or working practices.

The force field technique is especially useful when it is necessary to anticipate learning needs. People who analyse learning needs should, ideally, have access to any business plans that may exist, and in the absence of such plans you should gather information relevant to the business and be able to name planned or anticipated developments.

The force field provides one way of mapping the expected forces that could exist and in turn identifying any learning needs that can arise as a result. The technique is also used to analyse current developments, especially where a deadlock exists in adopting a new practice or technology. Although the necessary initiatives may be wide and varied, it is quite possible that learning needs will feature strongly.

The delphi technique

The delphi technique was developed by the Rand Organization in the United States of America during the early 1950s, primarily as a forecasting tool. It is used in a similar way when applied to the analysis of learning needs. The general aim is to present selected people with an issue that has implications for possible learning and then to forecast what the learning needs will be. For this reason delphi is used during the planning stage, rather than later when a new activity or process is already in place.

Delphi is linked to the nominal group technique (NGT) and both approaches use the principle of brainwriting. When people can be brought together in one place, it is preferable to use NGT rather than delphi. The delphi technique is particularly helpful when decisions about learning needs have to be made among people who are spread geographically, such as sales personnel, area managers or managers of smaller satellite operations.

The technique is administered by a coordinator and the analysis is conducted in seven steps (there can be more depending upon the number of questioning rounds):

1. Begin by stating the perceived need. Describe the changes or developments that are planned and suggest that learning needs could exist: 'From April next year, area managers will be responsible for running a profit-centre operation; it is expected that this will produce some learning needs.'
2. Select the managers to take part in the delphi exercise. They must be fully involved in the planned change, have time to devote to delphi and know how the technique works. The ideal number to select for such a sample is six to eight managers. This number makes it possible to come close to saturation. Delphi can be conducted with fewer people, but four is the minimum requirement.
3. Design a questionnaire that contains mainly open questions, asking for ideas about different aspects of the planned change as it is seen

to have implications for learning needs. It is helpful, at this stage, if an information gathering technique has been used to identify the main characteristics of the new working pattern, because the questions can be based partly on this information. Alternatively, a small group of managers can brainstorm some learning-related questions.

4. Next, pilot the questionnaire, using the same number of people as will be used in the delphi exercise, but not the managers in the sample. The piloting is designed to remove any ambiguity from the questions, to remove any questionnaire errors that may have crept in, and to check that the reading level of the questions is appropriate. The piloting method, set up at this stage, will be used again with a second or third delphi questionnaire at steps 6 and 7.

5. Send the questionnaire to the selected managers with a statement of the issues, and instructions to return the answers by a certain date.

6. When all the questionnaires have been collected, the coordinator, with assistance if necessary, analyses the responses and prepares a short report summarizing the collective ideas and views. Main ideas can be categorized under headings such as 'skills need', 'knowledge need', 'training course need', 'relationships' and so on. A second questionnaire is developed and piloted, the aim of which is to ask questions about any inconsistencies or misunderstandings, and to allow each manager the opportunity to respond to the ideas of others. Information is provided anonymously throughout the exercise, so managers do not know who has said what.

7. When the second questionnaire has been analysed, the coordinator may be able to produce a final report that details the findings and identifies the key areas for learning needs, the needs themselves and the preferred way of satisfying those needs. However, it is likely that a third round of questions will be needed, particularly to gather responses about priorities and preferred ways of learning. It is not unknown for four or five rounds of delphi to be used, but three is a realistic number and try to complete the report in two rounds if possible.

From a delphi exercise of this kind you should be able to arrive at a clear consensus about learning needs and support. The consensus comes from the people who will be fully involved in the new working practices. A common experience is that people attend training courses without having a clear idea about their exact purpose. When delphi, or a similar technique like NGT, is used, the participants become fully aware of the rationale behind the learning support decisions. When other managers are sent details of delphi and the reports and results, they too will share a clearer view of any training or other learning support that is offered.

Job analysis

Jobs are many and varied and generally grow erratically because they are tied up with the changing fortunes of organizations and are a central part of the institutionalization that occurs within organizations. Jobs are normally analysed by being broken down into identifiable 'chunks'. However, a vital part of any job performance are the behaviours that arise as a result of interactions between these 'chunks' of activity. The most common set of 'chunks' comprises functions, tasks and skills; though each in turn has its own analysis method, they form a part of any job analysis technique. These are shown in Figure 5.2 and to complete the break-down of the typical job, the level of abilities has also been included.

Every job consists of functions, that is a set of broadly defined operations that someone must perform if the job is to be done adequately. Some jobs such as an electronics board assembler may have no more than two functions of assembly and self-inspection. Other jobs such as nurse or police officer have many functions. It is difficult to identify learning needs at this level of analysis; try it.

Next, is the task level. Each function contains one or more tasks. A task is a well-defined act that has a clear start and finish point. An inspector on a production line may perform a 30-second checking task. A lawyer's briefing task may take an hour or more and will be one of a number of tasks within a function of preparing a case. To be a task, an activity must have a start and finish and must transform some kind of input into an output. It is possible to identify learning needs at this level, especially when changing the sequence of tasks, seeking to improve linkage between different tasks, or improving ways to prioritize tasks.

The final level most commonly reached is that of skills use. Each task can contain one or more skills. The task of styling hair includes the use of inter-personal behaviour (perceptual and cognitive skills), planning (cognitive skills), cutting (motor and perceptual skills) and forming (motor, perceptual and cognitive skills). The exploration of skills provides a productive level of analysis for the identification of learning needs. Knowing which area of skill use to explore if the task of styling has not been performed to the required standard greatly helps in the analysis of what needs to be learned. Analysis at this level can also reveal which skill areas cause the greatest learning difficulties and where learning support ought to be concentrated.

The most profound level of job analysis concerns abilities which are vital to the successful performance of a job. Jobs vary in the number and types of ability that are vital in this way. Using ability requirements can be a useful approach to the analysis of learning needs. The technique is most powerful where skills can be difficult to learn because the identification of areas of weakness in terms of abilities can help locate and focus learning needs. People who experience a restricted labour market because they have certain disabilities can be encouraged by helping them to locate strong abilities which can be utilized more fully.

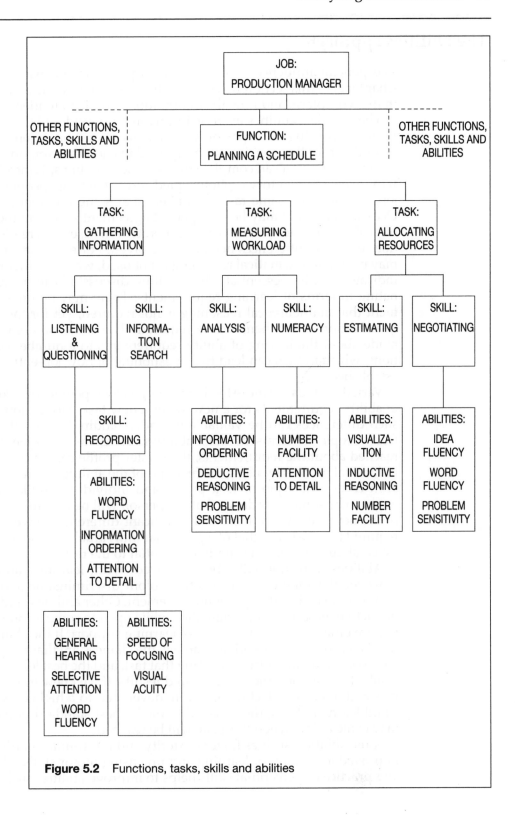

Figure 5.2   Functions, tasks, skills and abilities

The abilities approach

The general influence of our abilities upon learning was discussed in Chapter 2; in this section we see how the idea of abilities use can be applied in the workplace, and how the information is utilized to identify needs.

The two-part abilities exercise in Chapter 2 provides both an individual profile according to a person's own perception and a job profile. The second part of the exercise can be applied to a job that you do or a job you know well, or, you can complete the exercise thinking specifically of a task. If the exercise inventory is photocopied and given to ten people in the same job, or doing the same task, it is likely that some differences will occur. Occasionally there may be near perfect agreement and from the collection of profiles a master profile can be generated. In cases where disagreement does exist the differences need to be resolved. For example, one response may be that mathematical reasoning is not used, while another respondent indicates that it is essential. The resulting discussion can be quite illuminating in terms of learning requirements. There may be universal agreement that mathematical reasoning is not required, yet for the same job a qualification in mathematics is required. The same observation can be made about the linking of ability requirements to a number of qualifications, which in turn can lead to a questioning of how job-entry criteria are established.

Varied profiles are more likely to emerge when people are asked to think of ability requirements for a new job or a new task. Discussions to resolve such differences can be valuable in understanding what will be needed from people in terms of their abilities. When an agreement has been reached about the requirements, the master profile can be compared with individual profiles by using the first part of the abilities exercise in Chapter 2. In cases where job or task profile and individual profile match there ought to be some confidence that the person will be able to learn the skills of the new job. Where there is a significant difference between an ability required by a task and that of a particular individual a question needs to be asked about whether the ability is essential to the task.

Abilities can normally be improved with learning and practice, however, the abilities of rate control, colour discrimination and visualization seem to resist attempts at improvement. Other abilities of idea fluency, deductive reasoning and originality, while open to some improvement, do require quite sophisticated types of learning support. If the ability in question is one of the six mentioned above, the chances are that the person will have some real difficulty in learning that task and the best learning support available may not achieve the desired results. If we knew more about abilities and if learning technology were developed to a higher level, anyone could learn anything they wished to the highest standard possible. There may come a time when this state will be reached.

Some abilities, such as finger dexterity and multi-limb coordination, are improved as a result of learning and practising motor skills. The learning and practice of perceptual skills helps to improve abilities such as perceptual speed and visual acuity and the abilities of mathematical reasoning and information ordering can be improved through the learning and practice of cognitive skills. However, it is helpful to separate out certain abilities when you are faced with the analysis of learning needs for a skill that is particularly difficult to learn.

A training officer, for example, experiences some difficulty in achieving adequate results from a training programme designed to help operators adapt to a new semi-automated process. Despite using the normal task and training needs analysis in the design of the programme and receiving strong cooperation from operators, difficulties are experienced. By exploring abilities, the deepest level of job analysis can be reached, but it is not realistic for people in industry to probe further; to do so involves the analysis of abilities themselves. In this case, examination of the new process in terms of abilities may show, as is quite common with new technology, that an added demand exists for word fluency, to communicate complex process operations both orally and in writing in the form of record-keeping. Thus the ability of word fluency becomes a learning need and weakness in this ability can hinder the production process.

When people lose their jobs and begin looking for other forms of employment there is a tendency to look for jobs that match current skills. Various government bodies reinforce this view by emphasizing skills training. However, as discussed in Chapter 2, it is abilities rather than skills that transfer best between jobs. Emphasizing abilities as opposed to skills can open up a much wider horizon to people in their search for alternative employment. This view of transfer between jobs also supports those people who advocate lifelong learning. People have certain, well developed abilities that allow them to continue to learn skills into their seventies and eighties.

Unfortunately, data is not available to allow people to match their ability profile with a range of job profiles. If such data were available, people would be in a better position to place themselves within the labour market. Also, it is advantageous for organizations to be able to identify those abilities where learning can be said to have the biggest return. Where it can be clearly demonstrated, that some of the abilities being used are not receptive to cost effective training, then alternative means of employing these abilities has to be considered. This may place a greater emphasis upon staff selection, because the critical abilities being used are not responsive to training, education or other forms of learning.

AET

AET is an analysis technique developed in Germany. The abbreviation stands for '*arbeitswissenschaftliches Erhebungsverfahren zur Tätigkeitsanalyse*', or 'ergonomic job analysis' (Rohmert and Landau 1983). It provides insight into work where ergonomic issues are important. Approximately four thousand job analyses have been made using the technique.

A large number of industrial injuries and much work-related ill health may be contributed to by poor analysis of learning needs. In the past, the established methods of training needs analysis did not place sufficient emphasis upon the avoidance of physical and mental harm to people at work. A wider more holistic view must be taken of organizational work when analysing learning needs and this applies especially to ergonomic related issues. For example, journalism has suffered some quite serious incidents of repetitive strain injury as a result of the transfer to new technology. An appropriate analysis of motor skill use over time would highlight where such risks exist.

AET analyses three elements of a job:

1. The tasks.
2. The conditions under which each task is performed.
3. The resulting effects upon the person.

The first part of the analysis takes account of objects in the place of work. 'Objects' include any materials used (which could be harmful), information (which can be inadequate), people (a source of stress?) and so on. The second part of the analysis relates this information to how various objects are used and examines motor, cognitive and perceptual skill use. Finally a careful analysis is made of the effects upon people doing the work.

Ergonomic factors at work are closely linked to our perceptual, auditory, visual, tactile and olfactory senses. When these are examined in relation to the work to be done, the resulting information can lead to some significant changes. The changes are normally of three types:

1. A change in the design of equipment.
2. A change in processes and the way tasks are performed.
3. A change in the way people are taught.

It is the last type of change which has important implications for the analysis of learning needs. During the Second World War it was estimated that some four hundred RAF planes were lost as a result of human error. When the errors were analysed, it was found that a combination of equipment design and the need for particular skills learning accounted for most of them. It is also possible to recognize errors in the way people perform tasks at work, that lead not to poor quality work but instead to long-term physical injury. Only by taking a holistic view of the workplace, typically by adopting the three-part approach outlined here, is it possible to identify and so avoid injuries of this kind.

Errors, of any kind, are not necessarily eliminated with more skill or more practice; error-making is a quite separate issue from our use of skills. When assessing learning needs, the subject of errors at work has to be explored separately. Often, when people become gradually more skilled, they maintain their proportion of error-making. More skilled people can thus have a greater rate of error-making than less skilled people in the same job. Imagine a keyboard operator whose proportion of error-making remains constant as he or she becomes more skilled. More errors will be made per day when the operator is fully skilled because of the higher input. The operator may be experienced, but 'experience' in this sense refers to the performance of tasks at a greater speed and with greater confidence; there is no guarantee that the work will be error-free, or even that a reduction in error-making will occur.

There is a paradox here, because it may be felt that the longer someone is in a job, the less chance there will be that they continue potentially harmful practices, such as making errors in the use of a hand tool. Evidence shows that the longer someone is in a job, and hence the faster the rate of tool use, the worse become any earlier problems.

Data derived from AET exercises will not be in the form of clear learning needs, but will point to areas of concern where implications for learning needs exist. Details of the workplace that arise from the first part of the AET analysis may highlight a factor such as windows that do not open with the result that staff are dependent upon a mechanical ventilation system. This raises the question of what information people need in order to live happily with such conditions, given that they cannot be changed easily. Another area of concern could be the learning needs of people that will ensure effective operation of the mechanical system.

Workplace analysis also reveals issues linked to the learning needs of middle and senior managers, including the effects of open plan working, air flow, radiant heat, levels of illumination intensity, forms of seating and other possible sources of workplace hazards. Learning needs can be associated with a number of issues in the environment of offices and factories; the neglect of what needs to be known, or what skills are needed to overcome problems, can lead to the condition known as 'sick building syndrome' or to other harmful effects that take some time to be revealed. It is always questionable to name one factor as 'the cause' of a problem; there are usually many causes. Further workplace analysis may highlight sources of cause(s) that can lead to problems for the individual.

The second part of the AET analysis can reveal how tools or items of equipment are being used in a way that is ergonomically unsound. The analysis typically covers point-of-sale terminal use, computer operation, mechanical or physical loading/unloading methods and hand tool use.

The third part of the analysis concentrates upon what behaviours most affect the individual and it is here that various learning needs can be revealed. Potentially hazardous operations often have a knowledge need requirement and the way in which tools or equipment are being used can point to a skills need. As with the use of other techniques, this part of the analysis requires you to draw upon knowledge of skill use. Is the behaviour primarily one that involves mainly motor skill, or is there a strong reliance upon cognitive skill?

The AET technique has been specially developed to provide an analysis of the workplace and objects in the workplace for the purpose of analysing the learning needs of people with disabilities. This technique is referred to as D-AET.

Protocol analysis

Sometimes an appropriate learning need seems almost impossible to analyse. Think how you would help someone learn to become a more effective chess player. A common recommendation is to play progressively against opponents who are slightly 'better' players. There is a point at which chess players know how to play the game, the initial learning curve has levelled off and a new practice curve takes over; this applies to all skills that we learn and is illustrated in Figure 7.2 (see p. 92). If practice makes perfect, and practice is the one main variable then the person who puts in the most board-hours would be world chess champion. However, this is not the case and practice does not make perfect. It is the practice of effective learning that makes someone closer to perfect and it is the tapping of effective learning that poses the greatest difficulty; practice and experience come easily.

Many amateur chess players develop what they call a logical approach to the game. What they mean by logical is thinking along the lines of 'If I do this, then that is likely to happen and if that, then this and so on'. This type of thinking is normally combined with knowledge of the trade-off between the values of various pieces on the board. A break-through point is reached when some players begin to recognize patterns of play and their behaviour moves into a pattern recognition skill. The same developments can be observed in the behaviour of people who diagnose, such as medical doctors and engineering technicians. Analysis of the learning needs required to become an effective diagnostician is extremely difficult, certainly none of the conventional training needs analysis methods apply.

The technique of protocol analysis was developed to help in the identification of thought processes that lie behind skilled behaviour (Ericsson and Simon 1985). If we do not know what information is being used or how that information is being processed during the performance of a skilled task, how can we analyse learning needs for people who are unable to reach a required standard?

A protocol can be thought of as a set of rules that we have in our heads for processing 'chunks' of information. At a simple level, think of three people being asked to multiply 38 by 23 in their heads and to speak out loud as they do the calculation, do you imagine that they would use the same 'protocols'? Analysis of the three typescripts taken from recordings of the calculations would reveal differences in reasoning. From this type of analysis effective and less effective protocols can be recognized. The most effective approaches that are demonstrated often reveal the learning need of people who show less effective methods of processing in the particular task. Such information can be particularly valuable when analysing learning needs to improve skilled performance, as opposed to learning for the first time. Areas of work for which the technique is most appropriate include loss adjustment, insurance claim assessment, electronic fault diagnosis, financial loan decision-making and medical diagnosis. Protocol analysis can be used to analyse any task where complex or competing information has to be processed by a form of mental reasoning, to arrive at a solution.

Protocol analysis can take one of two forms: concurrent or retrospective. In the concurrent approach a skilled person talks through the performance of a skilled task while performing it. The investigator can either tape-record the session or take notes. The potential for needs identification is maximized when a number of typescripts taken from different people doing the same skilled task can be compared. Three engineers diagnosing the same fault may use different chunks of information, or protocols, in their respective reasoning. The analysis of these protocols and how they are used will usually reveal why one particular engineer is more effective at diagnosis than the other two. This information enables learning needs to be identified for other engineers who are much less effective. The same approach can be used with any skilled task where reasoning is an important part of the skill. Typical examples are airport check-in, police questioning, chemical plant start-up, silicon slice doping, electronic board quality checking, fashion design lay-out and computer programming.

The retrospective approach to protocol analysis takes the form of talking through a skilled task whilst not actually performing it. In jobs such as textile or newspaper production where there is much background noise this is often the only option. Again the sessions can be tape-recorded or notes taken. One problem with this approach is that respondents may fill in detail to justify their actions retrospectively and the spontaneity of the concurrent approach can be lost. A way around this is to combine the retrospective account with a technique of structured observation. To do this you observe the performance of the task on one occasion and then draw up a check-list of what you particularly want to note on the second occasion. When the second structured observation is complete, the information can be used in comparison with what is said during the retrospective account.

One session of protocol analysis may provide valuable data but more sessions are sure to illuminate skilled behaviour and lead to quite clear identification of what needs to be learned. However, this assumes that at least two or three people in the organization can provide examples of effective protocol use that contribute to their skilled behaviour. In some cases, such as radar waveguide development or expert system development, it may be that only one person of this kind is available and then it is hoped that the person concerned is happy to be milked dry of essential protocols. A textbook which deals specifically with protocol analysis has been written by Ericsson and Simon (1985).

Repertory grid

The underlying principles of repertory grid use are easy to understand and some useful pointers to needs analysis can be gathered as a result of applying the grid in its basic form. The central idea is that we all choose particular ways of constructing the 'reality' around us. We use terms of speech that both reflect the way we view reality and influence the way we interpret reality. If we were not individual in this respect then everyone who witnessed an event would give the same account of that event; we all know that this is not the case. In training programmes where case study material is used, the same case account of no more than 400 words will be interpreted differently by different course members, and a significant point will be noted by some members but not by others. Where typical constructs or terms that we favour appear in the script it is highly likely that we will focus quickly upon that kind of detail, while others may be overlooked.

The repertory grid technique can be used in two ways to help identify needs:

1. To check the consistency of people's constructs when they are describing the principal features of a process or a job.
2. To compare the way skilled people describe their behaviour and the behaviour of other skilled colleagues.

The technique was developed by George Kelly (Kelly 1985), and has been used and developed into what has become known as the personal construct theory. However, only the basic use of the grid is of interest here. A very good textbook (Stewart 1981) relates the repertory grid to business applications, and includes a section on its use in analysing learning needs.

The grid is based upon the idea that if we are forced to make comparisons between different events, between different people or different attitudes we will reveal some of the key constructs that help explain why we view that particular situation or person the way we do. Some people have more consistent sets of constructs than others, for example, if you say that Mary is more confident than either Kate or Henry, then the construct of 'confident' is applied in much the same way when either Kate or Henry is being considered; in other words your basic meaning behind the use of each construct holds true whatever the circumstances. For reasons that are not always clear, some people appear to use constructs in a quite inconsistent way and this can lead to some confusion when trying to analyse learning needs clearly.

The repertory grid works by thinking of three different items and saying in what particular way one of these items differs from the other two and in what way it is similar. The items can be three skilled people you know well, or three skilled tasks, or three views on quality perception. In describing differences and similarities between one skilled person Sally and two other skilled people John and Mary, a number of constructs may be used. John can then be compared in the same way with the other two, and finally Mary can be compared with John and Sally. The comparison can be extended to other groups of three people and in this way a quite comprehensive pattern of constructs can be established.

When a larger number of people are included, typically through the application of a repertory grid computer program, inconsistencies become apparent. Analysis of such information highlights constructs that can go some way to explaining differences and similarities in skilled performance. Imagine that the construct of 'reflective approach' and related constructs such as 'cautious' and 'checks well beforehand' were used whenever particularly skilled people were being discussed. Identification of these constructs allows us to then ask to what extent they can be recognized as a learning need for others.

The same technique can be applied to skilled tasks. A newly planned skilled task can be compared with two other established skilled tasks. If a small number of people who are very familiar with the area of work are asked to use the grid approach to say how the new task differs from an established task and then work through the three items as in the example above, much insight can be gained into essential differences and similarities. This analysis may reveal that elements of the skill needed for the new task already exist in the plant. Such insight can aid decisions as to what learning needs will be required when people transfer to the new task.

Another useful area of application is in comparing people's perception of what quality means to them. It is common for organizations to talk at length about quality and total quality, and assume that everyone uses the construct 'quality standard' in the same way. Given that inconsistency can be seen to occur *within* people in their use of constructs the chance is high that inconsistency will occur *between* people.

If a number of people are asked to use the grid approach to compare three quality measures or statements that are adopted by the company, much could be learned about different perceptions of quality. Most perceptions revealed in this way have implications for learning. Often the learning will be in the form of awareness-raising, in particular that some people have constructs that are consistent with those of the organization while others may display quite significant differences.

When a new working practice is introduced conflicting views may arise about what people will need in order to adapt and eventually perform effectively. There can be fairly predictable differences such as those between the designers of the new practice and those who will have the task of supervising it. When designing a training programme for new ways of working, the differences of view between supervisors, managers and those who will perform the skilled tasks can be disruptive and may lead to inappropriate learning needs being identified. Detailed knowledge about these differences can help us plan for the new work and the use of the grid can help clarify the nature of any differences.

Why consistency or inconsistency exists is a subject that the construct theory is typically applied to, but need not concern us here. It is sufficient to be aware that inconsistency in our use of constructs can exist and that by exploring them, through the use of the repertory approach, it is possible to achieve more clarity and understanding at work.

Skills analysis

When analysing skills we need to take account of what we know about abilities. Often, skills have been thought of as a quite separate part of human behaviour but we can only expect to understand the learning of skills in terms of the abilities that so strongly influence how we learn and eventually how we perform. If I decided to take up cricket as a pastime it would be in the knowledge that despite considerable practice, my batting skill could never be more than mediocre. Three of the abilities critical to the skill of batting, rate control, body orientation and multi-limb coordination, are weak in my case. Other necessary abilities of dynamic strength, flexibility of movement and selective attention are quite strong but do not compensate for the other weaknesses. In contrast, skilled performers in this area have all these abilities developed to a high level, partly in an innate way and partly as a result of learning and practice.

The effective skills analyst must be able to identify when cognitive, motor or perceptual skill are being used, whether separately or in combination. Another requirement is to know when related knowledge is an indispensable part of a skill being used. For example many people use the skill of driving with little or no knowledge of how a vehicle works, and the same is true of the use of computers. Two important points should be noted about the link between skills and knowledge: a skill can or cannot be performed without certain knowledge, and while the skill can be performed under ideal conditions without knowledge this may not apply in abnormal conditions. While many people may be able to perform a skill under stable conditions, whenever the unexpected occurs difficulties are best handled by people who have an *understanding* of the process.

It is in this respect that the basic statements of what people can do prove inadequate, because they are based upon product or output rather than upon process and understanding. A feature of new technology development is that knowledge, and the understanding that comes through the effective practice of knowledge, has become an increasing need. This need can be summarized in the word 'scholarship', an unfashionable term. However, it is to this use of knowledge that members of governments are probably referring when they complain that the general educational level is inadequate for the demands of the latest technology. One message here is that current uses of skill in the workplace can seldom be discussed or assessed without regard to possible key knowledge and understanding.

Skills analysis is performed most effectively when the investigator can state the following:

- Describe clearly the types of skill being used.
- Identify the abilities that are critical to the learning and to the performing of each type of skill.
- State how abilities that are difficult to influence through learning may hinder the development of the skills.

- State how far knowledge and understanding are essential in the normal performance of the skills.
- State essential requirements when the skills have to be performed under abnormal conditions.

SWOT

The technique of SWOT has become well known in recent years, and with the now commonly used techniques of brainstorming and survey is part of a move towards the use of multiple techniques. SWOT is based upon a simple matrix, with strengths and weaknesses (SW) described in the two top squares and opportunities and threats (OT) in the bottom two squares (hence SWOT), as shown in Figure 5.3. When people are faced with a new process, a new piece of machinery, a new marketing strategy or having to adapt methods of working, this technique can be used to highlight possible learning needs. In Chapter 10 there is a further explanation of this technique, together with an example of practical application.

The first step is to gather information about the planned change, ideally using an investigative technique for information gathering. People are asked to use this information to list what they consider to be the particular strengths that will allow them to meet the change confidently. They are then asked to list what they consider to be weaknesses that could lead them to approach the change with some apprehension. At this point it is a

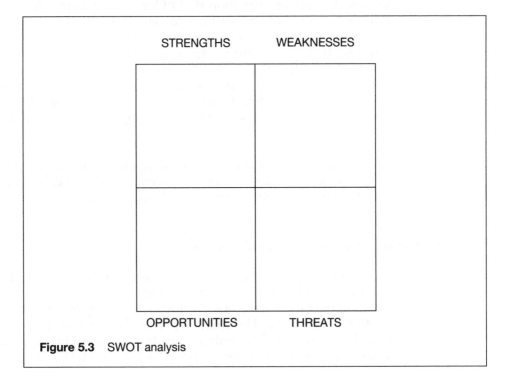

Figure 5.3   SWOT analysis

good idea to look at the list of weaknesses to see whether some can be re-framed into strengths. For example, 'reluctance to switch tasks regularly' can read, 'able to concentrate upon a task in great detail'. Wherever possible, a positive side has to be found in what are seen as weaknesses. Unalterable weaknesses that will influence the changed patterns of working are explored for opportunities to correct them. Within these opportunities there are normally clues to some form of learning need. An 'inability to handle spreadsheets related to cost control' could reveal a need to be more numerate and thus identifies a learning need. Each listed weakness is explored in this way.

The opportunities that people see arising from the change can lead to learning needs. If part of a new marketing strategy includes exploiting the opening up of the EC, then language learning and related learning about business culture becomes an apparent need. When such opportunities have been recognized it is a good idea to use another technique such as delphi, storyboard, or skills analysis to bring out possible learning needs in more detail.

The 'threats' often concern apprehensions that people have when faced with change of any kind. When changes have implications for the use of skills and knowledge, there can be feelings of inadequacy. The worst outcome would be for such feelings to remain hidden. It is factors such as this that are typically removed from an AET analysis, because the threats can have a detrimental effect upon people both physically and mentally. When the threats are discussed openly, they can be re-framed into opportunities. The mis-information that older people cannot learn certain new skills may cause older workers to feel threatened by any change that demands new skills, but statements in the 'threats square' can be transferred to the 'opportunities square' by encouraging people to accept the idea of lifelong learning.

At the end of the SWOT exercise the opportunities square should contain at least one identification of a learning need. Needs may also arise from the strengths square, that is, learning in order to build on already recognized strengths. Other possible learning needs can arise from the weaknesses square.

The SWOT analysis is of more benefit when combined with at least one other technique. It can be used very well as part of a delphi approach that allows for wider dissemination and decision-making.

The nominal group technique (NGT)

The nominal group technique was developed by Andre Delbecq and Andrew Van de Ven (Van de Ven and Delbecq 1971). It involves an exercise not dissimilar to Delphi, but conducted with a group of people gathered together in one place. The analysis process is therefore quicker when using NGT. The use of NGT for training needs assessment in the United States of America has been described by Scott and Deadrick (1982).

NGT is conducted in a series of steps:

1. Each person in a group, ideally of between six and ten members, is given a sheet of paper with a statement about an event that has prompted the anticipation of possible learning needs. This is often referred to as a statement of the problem, but I prefer to look upon tasks of this kind as challenges rather than as problems. This statement can follow the lines of that used at the beginning of the delphi technique (see p. 56). In silence, and for about ten minutes, each person thinks about the statement and writes as many ideas as they can on the sheet of paper.
2. When idea writing has been exhausted, a person acting as the coordinator writes one idea from each person on a whiteboard or large sheets of paper so that everyone can view them. Each idea is numbered sequentially as recorded, for easy reference later.
3. Next, each idea is discussed. No one should feel that their idea has to be defended, the aim is to have an open consideration of each idea that has been submitted. Additions to ideas can be made and the coordinator writes down further comments.
4. When the discussions are over, another silent period follows while each person ranks the ideas in order of priority. The criterion for this has to be agreed beforehand, for example, 'the priority in which learning need or learning support should be tackled'. Another criterion could be, 'what is most critical to the individuals concerned', or 'what is most critical to the organization', if in the unlikely event, the two are not the same.
5. Finally, the rankings from each person are recorded by the coordinator and hopefully the priority areas for attention will become clear.

From an NGT exercise involving six people it can be expected that around 15 to 20 ideas will be generated and that at least two will go forward as serious needs to be supported.

The cartoon storyboard technique

The cartoon storyboard technique was developed in the United Kingdom by Jane Henry at the Open Business School (OBS). Reference to the technique can be found in part of the OBS MBA programme called 'Creative Management'. Like many effective techniques, this one is simple.

The cartoon storyboard exercise begins with a large sheet of paper on a wall, visible to everyone involved. The sheet is divided into six squares of equal size. The next stage is to think about the event that has prompted you to consider possible learning needs. This can be a new process, a new product or a new working pattern; it can also be better performance of some kind. It helps greatly if during this exercise you, and any colleagues involved, are in a relaxed state of mind and body. At the very least, there must be no interruptions of any kind. The first task is to imagine the desired outcome of the event being considered. What does the picture of 'ideal' actually look like? What will it feel like? Who will be involved? What is the goal? When you have a picture in your mind, draw this in the last box (6) on the sheet. Be free and imaginative, draw stick figures, places, products, connections – everything you can think of that illustrates what for you is the ideal situation.

When you are happy with this picture of the 'ideal', bring your mind back to the current situation; in the case of the planned event, this is the starting point. Now, as before, imagine what best illustrates the present with respect to the planned change. What does 'now' look like? Who is involved? What connections are there? When this picture is clearly in mind, draw it in the first box (1).

The next stage is to complete pictures for boxes 2 to 5. What needs to be done first in moving away from the present position? What will this scene look like? This is repeated for each of the remaining boxes, as a progression to the ideal state. Spend some time thinking about what you have produced; does the board give a realistic picture of where you are, where you are going and some ideas about how to get there? After any necessary modifications, you are ready to examine each box in turn for the main challenges that have to be overcome, or the principal tasks that need to be achieved; write these under each box. It is from this reflection stage that implications for learning needs can emerge. The comments under the boxes are often of certain blocks to progress, from where you are to where you want to be, and these blocks can consist of such terms as lack of necessary skill, of knowledge, or necessary learning support.

Ideally, you use the technique by yourself when involved in the analysis of learning needs, but contributions from one or two other colleagues can be included. One of the best approaches is for colleagues to complete the same exercise independently, then come together to compare finished results and to pool the best ideas.

It is not difficult to see how this technique can be used effectively by anyone who wishes to analyse personal learning needs. Identifying where you are now occupationally, where you wish to be and what ought to be done to get there can reveal what skills and knowledge will be required to achieve that end.

Selecting techniques

The techniques for analysis that have been described are complementary to the techniques of information gathering discussed in the previous chapter. Before any analysis of learning needs can begin, you need to describe clearly the event that has brought even the slightest hint that learning may be needed. This descriptive part utilizes the information gathering techniques. Before you chose the technique(s) for analysis you should have gathered all relevant information about the event or change. In Table 5.1

the two types of technique are shown together, as they relate to typical events.

The choice of technique(s) should also be guided by what you know about the skills, knowledge and abilities that will be involved; either based upon your own knowledge or using the information provided in earlier parts of this book.

These techniques are normally used on two different occasions when analysing learning needs. First, when people are making a diagnosis for the purpose of making some changes or in order to bring about some improvements in performance at work. Second, when learning needs are being linked to longer-term strategic planning. In the latter case, the information and the analysis that results serves two functions: to extract from the plan, clear implications for future learning needs, and to feed current analysis about learning needs into business planning. The subject of linking business plans to learning needs is covered in Chapter 10.

As a guide to help in the choice of techniques, Table 5.1 shows the relationship between events that can prompt the need for learning and the techniques used to gather information and for analysis. The matrix is not to be treated rigidly; the techniques are linked to the events which seem most appropriate. Also, when gathering information about any one event it is likely that only one technique will be used, so a choice needs to be made from those techniques recognized as most appropriate, and the same is true for analysis techniques.

Table 5.1   The relationship between events and technique use

	Technique
	A = Listening and questioning
	B = Critical incident technique
	C = Brainstorming/brainwriting
	D = Survey questionnaire
	E = Force field analysis
	F = Delphi
	G = Job analysis
	H = Abilities approach
	I = AET
	J = Protocol analysis
	K = Repertory grid
	L = Skills analysis
	M = SWOT
	N = Nominal group technique
	O = Cartoon storyboard

Event	A	B	C	D	E	F	G	H	I	J	K	L	M	N	O
Promotion	*						*	*					*		*
Side-ways movement	*						*	*				*	*		
A new job	*						*	*				*	*		*
Introducing a new technology	*	*	*		*	*			*	*		*	*		
Introducing a new working method	*	*	*	*	*									*	*
Introducing a new process	*	*			*	*	*				*	*		*	
A move to multi-skilling	*	*			*	*		*	*			*	*		
A move to dual-skilling	*	*			*	*		*	*			*	*		
Introducing flexible working	*	*			*	*		*	*	*		*	*		
Improving skills and knowledge	*	*		*				*	*	*		*	*		
Loss of market share	*		*	*	*	*								*	*
Take-over	*	*			*	*		*						*	*
Move to home-based working	*	*		*	*	*	*	*	*		*	*	*		*
Move to part-time working	*			*	*		*	*	*						
Flatter organizational structure	*			*	*	*					*			*	*
Move to semi-automated process	*	*			*	*	*	*	*			*			*
Reduced/expanded staff numbers	*			*	*			*	*	*		*	*		
Move to employ older workers	*	*			*		*	*	*		*	*	*		*
Re-allocation of responsibilities	*	*	*				*	*			*	*			*

6 Taking account of changing work practices

Self-diagnosis

Begin this section by referring to Table 5.1 on the facing page. Study the event table of the matrix for a while to see if you can think of other events that are not included. Then think of those events that you have experienced, and for each one think about any additional learning that arose as a result of the event. In those cases where learning was required, think about how well training needs were analysed and carried through. Do this before reading on any further.

One of the factors that would make your response to this exercise either positive or negative would be the way that the events in question were anticipated. If the learning need was planned, and support such as training was provided in advance of the event, this would go some way to compensating for any lack of quality in the actual training when delivered. If the planning was followed by effective and efficient training then this ought to have been a rewarding experience. On the other hand, if the need identification and support was produced in reaction to the event it is likely that your experience will have been a negative one, mainly because there is every probability that the training was inappropriate. When the analysis of learning needs is conducted badly, or not at all, any training will be inappropriate; the training itself may be excellent but it will be of doubtful value if it is not matched to well-identified needs. Also, a reactive response as opposed to a planned response is very likely to lead to an inappropriate analysis of needs and thus eventual support will be inappropriate too.

The reaction of some people to a plea for more planning is to say, 'It's fine on paper, all this talk about planning, but at the coal face things are different, we don't have time to be proactive.' Such views are widespread. This attitude to planning for learning needs can apply even where the changes are internal to the organization and are fully within the control of management. When working practices are changed, or when new technology is introduced, the subject of learning tends to be put on one side for future discussion. Has this happened in your own experience?

Events that trigger learning needs may not be entirely within the control of the management; some events are a result of external influences. For example, a re-organization after take-over or a loss of market-share, can lead to rapid developments that leave little or no time for the analysis of learning needs and the provision of support. A reactive response to learning needs may appear to be justified in such situations. If you have had an experience of this kind, check back through the process to see whether learning needs could have been anticipated and responded to appropriately. Perhaps you are in the throes of such an event and can think of typical responses to this subject from those around you.

The idea that some events lead inevitably to reactive responses needs to be examined closely, because some organizations do manage to anticipate changes very well, and plan accordingly. In such circumstances there are often people who keep their eyes and ears wide open. Such people, who have a feel for trends in the changing patterns of work, the latest developments in technology and movement in the labour market, find it easier to anticipate any likely developments and changes nearer to the home base.

You have been thinking about past or current events in your own working life and what typical responses are made towards the analysis of learning needs and support. Now, think about events which could occur in the next two years in your organization. If you have access to a business plan it may provide useful clues. Also, think about the main external influences upon the organization and whether any events are likely to influence some of your working practices. In other words divide the likely events into two types:

1. Those developments that could take place entirely within your own organization and which are under the control of management.
2. Those developments that could take place outside the boundary of your organization and may not be within your control, but can influence current working practices.

In order to examine effectively developments outside the organization, you need to have an awareness of what is happening in various other areas not related to your own. So, complete the following exercise now:

1. Name, if you can, at least one likely internal development and describe how any learning needs will be analysed and eventually supported.

2. Name at least one anticipated outside development that could influence your organization and think about how learning needs would be analysed and supported.
3. Name at least one development that is not linked to your area of work but which is of some interest to you, and try to imagine how learning needs would be analysed and supported.

It may be helpful to draw up a table of events that are internal, external and of interest to you and in each case make notes about possible learning needs and the kinds of support that could be required.

If you cannot think of developments that could bring about learning needs, then it would appear that in your case most learning needs and support will be identified for the purpose of improving skills and knowledge, rather than in anticipation of likely future developments. The subject of analysing needs and support for the purpose of performance improvement is covered later.

Thinking about developments both within and outside the workplace in this way can increase awareness of the highly volatile nature of current working practices. In other words, events should not suddenly arrive on the organization's doorstep like unexpected guests that leave you scurrying around making rapid alterations to planned activities. When this does happen and the outcome is not disastrous then your organization has been fortunate. Often the lack of planning for learning needs has negative repercussions that will linger for some time.

When you have read the case studies in the next section of this chapter, think back to the responses you have given in this diagnostic section. As a result, you may be able to make links between the experience of others and your own current experience. It appears that one block to learning about learning is that people assume that their experience is unique; surely no experience is unique and there is an enormous amount that can be learned from the learning experience of others, no matter how different their work appears to be from your own.

Case studies of changing work practices

This section aims to provide different approaches to the analysis of learning needs and support through the use of examples of changes to working practices.

Four examples are provided:

1. Skill change within health care.
2. Developing a multi-discipline project team.
3. Identifying skills for new technology in printing.
4. Learning to weld.

In the example from health care, policy changes have led to the addition of certain cognitive skills where previously motor and perceptual skills had predominated. The next example deals with a technology-driven change to working practices, which in turn resulted in inter-relationship skills in team-building becoming important. A further example of technology-driven change is provided but this time the emphasis is upon the transfer of skill use from essentially motor skills to cognitive skills. The last example explores the difficulties that can be encountered in the analysis of learning needs; in this example the emphasis is upon motor skill use. In the examples frequent references are made to the use of techniques as part of building a strategy for analysing learning needs, and practical examples of such a strategy in use are provided.

Changes in health care practice

This first example concerns an event that resulted in changes to health care working practices. The changes occurred in a large health authority and have been repeated a number of times in the past five years.

When thinking about planning for learning needs it helps to be quite clear about the forces that are driving such changes and what forces could be resisting them, if any. The technique of force field analysis is a very illuminating way of setting the scene for the analysis of learning need. In this case the main driving force was a need to give nursing staff greater responsibility for managing their own resources and processes, in short, to come close to being business managers. The main resisting force was the perception that many staff had of nursing as being primarily concerned with care which, it was felt by many, could come into conflict with a preoccupation about business concerns. Both forces described here, along with others that were recognized, had implications for the analysis of learning needs.

Part of Lewin's force field theory is that it becomes necessary to reduce the restraining forces or increase the driving forces if the desired event is to take place. This often results in learning needs in the form of increasing awareness, developing a new skill, picking up new knowledge and understanding or adapting to a new process. In this particular case it had to be established whether training or some other learning support could contribute to a reduction in the not inconsiderable restraining forces and thereby smooth the way for a successful adoption of the new working practices.

When proposed changes in working practices come into conflict with in-built perceptions about the job, you need to take a step back and ask what learning is needed in preparation for the change. This contrasts to any learning that may be needed in order to *implement* the changes. In some cases this step is not taken and the usual outcome is that people retain their resentment to any of the new ideas and this can have a bad effect on any planned training. In this case the learning needs were analysed in clear recognition of the conflicting forces and provided an example of conflict being used in a constructive way. In addition to the identification of driving and resisting forces, three other techniques were used: critical incident, simulation and development centre.

Critical incident was chosen because the proposed changes affected the behaviour of people quite specifically. Also, the new working practices being planned were novel in this area of work; information had to be gathered from accountants, budget controllers, administration managers and more senior health department personnel about how the new practices would be performed. The use of critical incident allows people to recognize quickly the most important elements and enables them to describe behaviours; without such a technique it can be difficult to articulate what needs to happen to make the practices work effectively.

From this information it became clear that nursing staff would need to perform tasks new to them. At this point a simulation was used to allow people to sample examples of the new working practices. One important new task was to interpret budget figures in a spreadsheet format. With the help of people in finance and the critical incident information they provided, a simulated exercise was designed that included the essential skill and knowledge needed to perform this task. The abilities required in this case were selective attention, flexibility of focusing, number facility and problem sensitivity. This exercise, along with others, was undertaken by nursing officers as part of a development centre over a period of two days.

A development centre is based upon the principle of the assessment centre which is used by some companies to select personnel. However, running a development centre is quite different. Although the development centre includes a period of learning when all necessary information is provided in support of each simulation exercise, there is no pass or fail; it is entirely diagnostic.

When each exercise had been completed, the nursing officer talked through the experience with a more senior staff member and the outcome for each officer was that either a considerable learning need existed, some learning was needed, or the officer felt confident that this part of the planned change could be made without difficulty. At the conclusion of all the exercises a fourth outcome was possible – that the new way of working would be unacceptable to an officer. In this respect, the analysis of learning needs had been unsuccessful in reducing restraining forces to the new working practices. However, the centre had provided ample evidence for such a view and a move for that person to another area could be fully justified.

The practical simulated exercises, being diagnostic, allow for the identification of skills that need developing or improving, and identify where additional knowledge has to be provided or at least the source of access made known. The people involved in this needs analysis exercise had also experienced the main parts of the new working practices in advance of their implementation. The confidence that came from knowing, in advance, that they could either fulfil the requirements of the new practices or had the means of learning to fulfil them helped overcome a good deal of the initial resistance. At times we doubt our ability to cope with new practices and such doubt often drives our resistance.

Following the exercises, learning support was provided in the form of training programmes that were based upon further simulated practice, further guidance by a senior person and controlled discovery learning as the practices were implemented.

The multi-discipline project team

The event to be described here took place in a heavy engineering manufacturing organization and was driven by changes in technology. Before the introduction of the microprocessor, design work and the production of drawings were done by draughtspersons working individually at drawing boards, as in most manufacturing companies. Each skilled person worked within a specific area depending upon whether their particular discipline was mechanical, electrical, construction or architecture. Draughtspersons performed most of their working tasks at the drawing board and owned a chest of drawing equipment; a kind of 'find it' chest. The event which was to change these practices was the introduction of computer-aided design (CAD) that eventually linked-in to computer-aided manufacture (CAM). These two aspects of computer use, when combined with computer-aided planning (CAP) and computer-aided quality (CAQ) form a system of computer-integrated manufacturing (CIM). When it is fully developed and established in the next five to ten years, CIM will have further implications for the analysis of learning needs which do not appear to have been adequately explored. If your field is manufacturing you may like to reflect back to the diagnostic section in this chapter to see whether this kind of development was included in your thinking.

As a result of the CAD–CAM event many of the standard and routine calculations were speeded up considerably and people began to think of ways to integrate the work of these various disciplines into more creative tasks. Time could now be used for people to work together and produce in teams, more creative solutions to design problems. Some fairly clear learning needs existed in connection with CAD–CAM software use and procedures for networking with other departments and other parts of the organization. Less clearly defined were learning needs associated with working through a keyboard, as opposed to the use of a technical skill in the use of draughting instruments.

It was often said that technical draughtspersons, although artists in their own right, are frustrated creative artists. Their position is similar to that of the creative writer who makes the transfer from pen or pencil to the practice of working directly with a word processor. A feature of the creative process is that generally the least interference there is between the person and the ideas arriving on paper, or some other medium, the better. At present this remains a problem and one solution is to work on the creative part of the task by hand before applying the finishing touches by machine, in this case a computer workstation. How draughtspersons and writers think on the keyboard is a skill that eludes some people and we need to know more about the skill in terms of abilities before adequate learning support can be designed. We need to capture the pattern of thinking that aids the transfer of ideas directly to computer input. One of the best investigative techniques for a task of this kind is protocol analysis, because it allows for essential thinking (cognitive) processes to be revealed. When such information has been gathered, it can be shared through the use of the delphi technique as a means to reach a decision about the precise type of learning that is needed.

Another area of possible learning need in this situation concerns the building of relationships between the three main roles in any new project team arrangement. The principal role is that of team leader; unlike a manager role this can be rotated among certain team members depending upon the type of project. The second role is that of the team members, they are drawn from different disciplines and often from different departments for the duration of the project, whether for six weeks, six months or a year. The third role is that of line manager; while the project-team members report to the leader all will also have other lines of reporting to their respective managers. The management of this three-way relationship is vital to the success of any project team, and the people in each role have shared learning needs with each other. In some cases this is not recognized and a likely outcome, as happened here, is that some line managers feel isolated and not in control of their staff who are seconded to the project teams. One possible solution to this problem of divided loyalties is the establishment of venture teams (Holt 1991), that are more autonomous in their working but often require a significant change to be made in management style. Again, different learning needs arise as a result of this approach, for example there is a need to consider programmes of education as well as training support.

In this case it seemed sensible that learning about how to operate in a team was best conducted in the team, similarly the best way to analyse learning needs ought to be within a team. For these reasons, it was desirable to use at least one group technique as part of the strategy for analysing learning needs. One solution would have been to use the brainstorming technique with the team, to highlight what was needed to overcome relationship problems associated with project working. Unfortunately this technique, while an immensely valuable aid to problem-solving, is not ideal for relationship problems. Some people can feel inhibited by others in the group and as a result a free flow of ideas is not generated. To overcome this problem the delphi technique was used. Through the use of this technique the facilitator was able to highlight the main misunderstandings and behaviours that made relationships difficult and hindered the work of teams, and at times resulted in going over budget or over time on projects. The main learning needs identified were in the form of raising awareness and the extension of networking skill to people outside the teams so that they could be better informed of developments.

The delphi technique was also used to explore the learning needs of team members. An important need among team members was the means to encourage more than two or three members to be creative in their work, that is, to allow for the generation of ideas from more than typically a team leader and one or two other members. The belief that people can learn to be more creative and generate more ideas is still controversial, but, a first step is to be able to identify where the need exists, what types of skill and knowledge are involved and what abilities are used by people who do display such skill and knowledge. It may even be that the time is fast approaching when our knowledge about abilities and the learning technology at our disposal will lead to anyone being able to learn anything, and the concept of genius will become obsolete.

Other learning needs can be associated with project team working, such as how team members adapt to regular liaison with a range of clients. This form of team-working is increasing in many different kinds of operation and the development of a strategy to analyse needs and support in this area appears to be a necessity.

The introduction of new print technology

In this example the need to learn arose because after five hundred years of steady technological development in the print industry a revolution occurred that made many printing skills obsolete. The technology was developed in the early 1970s, but for a number of reasons did not have an impact upon skill use until the mid-1980s. Since then there have been significant changes to working practices and in some respects the industry can be used as a model for the effects brought about by the introduction of microprocessing.

It was technology that provided the initial driving force for the change. A first step towards recognizing needs in this case was to use the force field technique. From the information gathered in this way it became clear that changes in skill and knowledge use were inevitable and that the types of skill to be used would change dramatically. The next step in analysing learning needs was to describe the new skills in terms of the behaviours that would be demonstrated by people in the new jobs. The main shift was from motor skill to cognitive and perceptual skills, and people would be working in small multi-discipline teams.

Where totally new ways of working are being introduced, an expected source of learning support is the provider of the technology, however, in many cases this expected support turns out to be weak or non-existent. Sceptics often point out that providers of new technology are unlikely to supply effective learning back-up because it is not in their interests to do so; there can be more lucrative returns in helping to maintain the new operations. Possibly nearer the truth is that it is difficult to define the skills, abilities, and types of learning that are needed. In a competitive market place there appears to be a missed opportunity when manufacturers do not design and supply learning support as part of the contract. In the case described here the manufacturers followed the familiar pattern of emphasizing what their hardware and software could do, and neglected what people would be required to do when adapting to the new equipment and practices. An outcome of this is that although the equipment will work, its potential is seldom fully exploited because the technology that has been designed to help people respond and adapt to the new process is not sufficiently emphasized. The inability of organizations fully to exploit advances in new technology, as a result of neglecting learning needs and the attendant support for individuals, must be seen as a significant contribution to industrial and commercial inefficiency.

It was the printing organization, customers and users of the new technology, that had to take the lead in identifying the skills and knowledge that would be required. They also designed the necessary training after this had been recognized as the best way for people to gain these skills and knowledge.

The strategy for this work consisted of three techniques and a programme that was divided into three phases. The technique of critical incident was used to identify the behaviours that were vital to effective performance and from this an analysis was given of the precise types of skill being used. The abilities approach was then used as a technique to help explain, diagnostically, where any difficulties in learning might occur. Finally the technique of simulation was used as part of a trainability programme to help identify who would be most trainable in the various tasks. The simulations were also used as a means of training on the job.

The three phases of the programme consisted of the analysis of behaviours, skills and abilities, then the selection of people for training by the use of trainability tests, and finally the development of training programmes. Unlike other selection tests of the psychometric type, the use of trainability allows for performance on the tests to be diagnostic. This is because it is practical, and it is possible to identify where learning need exists in performing a particular skill during a test.

Trainability tests consist of short simulated practical exercises that take between 20 and 30 minutes to perform. The normal approach is to select a task within a job that can be said to be most critical in terms of what needs to be learned. The principle being applied is that if someone can demonstrate the ability to learn this particular task, then it can be predicted with some confidence that the person will be able to learn the other tasks too. Trainability differs from other tests in that the test is preceded by a period of instruction; it is for this reason that the result of the test is a measure of trainability, or how well the person can be expected to learn when given training. When, on the other hand, it is necessary to know if someone can do a particular task, as opposed to learning it, then a job sample test is used. In the case of new print technology, tasks were being introduced that were unknown to many people in the industry and the use of trainability allowed people to discover how trainable they would be in the new roles.

In any situation where new technology is being introduced for the first time, there is value in simulating the most significant tasks as a means of diagnosing the skills in terms of what needs to be learned, and who will be most able to learn.

By using a strategic approach to the identification of learning needs and support, the same attention and rigour is applied to aspects of human performance that is normally reserved for the implementation and use of new hardware and software.

Learning to weld

Welding, apart from being an activity vital to the well-being of any industrial country, provides a fascinating subject for the identification of learning needs and support. Possibly the main reason for this fascination is that so few people are able to reach the standards necessary for work of exceptional quality on projects such as nuclear power plants or offshore oil and gas operations. In one centre known for its excellence in welding technology it is not unknown for a ratio of 200:6 to exist between people who complete the courses and those who attain a required top standard. The development of new technology throws up similar problems around the subject of analysing real learning needs. In the area of systems analysis, knowledge engineering and process line operation, for example, there are serious difficulties in specifying and supporting learning needs.

In this section we are going to explore some ideas about the subject of welding and its learning. It may be that you have little interest in the subject of welding, but clear comparisons can be made between explorations of this kind and the learning needs of other complex skills. I use the word 'explore' deliberately because at present there is no means of adequately analysing learning needs in this area. A good deal of training in various subjects is based upon observation of what a skilled person can do; in the case of welding this is not possible. Also, a very complex interaction exists between the various abilities that are believed to influence the learning of this skill.

The abilities approach technique has been used to identify five abilities critical to the learning of the skill of welding: rate control, colour discrimination, gross arm control, general hearing and body orientation. If analysis of learning need reveals that a lack of colour discrimination seriously hinders the step from average standard welder to fully coded welder, then little is known of any training that could remedy this situation. Given that 8 per cent of males and 1 per cent of females are colour blind, there is an expectation that some male welders will have difficulty in this respect. Rate control is another ability where little is known about how to bring improvement through training. For this reason the abilities approach technique is seen as vital in any further learning needs analysis in this area.

A second appropriate technique is protocol analysis, which together with an awareness about abilities, can help skilled welders articulate the critical skilled behaviour. At the time of writing it is anticipated that multimedia aided simulation of the critical abilities will provide a means of overcoming blockages to the learning of this skilled work. Conventional training needs analysis has proved to be quite fruitless in the study of welding skills and a fresh approach is needed.

The principles and lessons that emerge from these cases can be applied to many other examples, but in each new case there may well be an unexpected twist to how people react and where a shift has to be made in analysing the necessary learning needs. From these examples I hope that the case for a strategy rather than a method of training needs analysis has been made.

Trends in changing work practices

The exploration of new working practices will now continue in a more general way so that broader examples can be provided of the changes going on around us.

Most organizations in western industrialized countries will have to adapt to an ageing population. The response of some companies has been to meet this trend head-on by recruiting older people. Where this has happened it is likely that significant learning needs will exist of a kind that is different to that of a younger workforce. Research suggests that older people need to learn in a different way and that such learning can be as effective as that of much younger people. The results from skilled performance in cognitive, motor and perceptual tasks shows that a group of younger people will perform faster and more effectively than a group of older people. However, there are greater performance variations *within* each age-group than there are *between* the older and younger groups. In other words some older people can perform much more effectively than some younger people.

It is not age itself that determines learning performance but *how* people age. One important factor that clouds the age and learning issue is illness. Because certain illnesses that hinder the learning process are more common among older people there will be more learning difficulties within an older group. However, the illness factor should not be allowed to confuse our thinking about how older people learn. I know of a man in his early seventies who is involved in business, lectures to business students, has taught himself computer programming and is beginning work on expert-system use. Another seventy-year-old is completing a book, making a video and travels the world on business. Many Open University students of this age and older work on quite complex learning tasks on degree programmes, or as associate students. For people in organizations who are charged with analysing learning needs this trend towards the older worker provides a new challenge, but existing methods are not equipped to cope with the complexity of this challenge.

Another significant trend in working practices is the move out of the organization and into the home, although, inexplicably, organizations continue to build large office blocks in central locations. The predictions of Alvin Toffler (1971) have been realized over the past ten years, but still the building continues and as Toffler also predicted the accommodation is, in places, being converted into domestic housing. This shift of working practices into the home presents yet another problem in analysing learning needs and support for people who work at home. Many people currently perform their tasks within the institutional atmosphere of organizations with all the support that implies; the step to independent working brings a number of new learning needs.

Six categories of home-worker can be identified and each may require a different approach to learning needs analysis (see Figure 6.1). In the case of one person who changed to being effectively self-employed under the guidance of his company the response was that 'The training I needed I did not take and the training I took I did not need'. Another factor is the complex relationship that arises, for the husband or wife, with the 'home networker'. Networking, if the relationship needs are clear and the learning needs and support are well handled, can result in a stronger family unit. Unfortunately seriously strained relationships can develop when one, or both, partners have an involvement in work-based networking from the home.

An interesting aspect of home-working is that as the trend increases the method of working will become a model for children growing up in such households. Perhaps a new generation will grow up expecting such work patterns to be the norm.

Another aspect of home-working where learning is important occurs when a person spends some time working away from home in other people's offices and then returns mentally to their office rather than to home. Without attention to the physical layout and associated handling of family relationships, this is an easy trap into which to fall. Broking skills become important to most home-workers. Even if they are linked to a company they need to sell what is done at home, and the company contact also needs to learn how to handle this new role as a buyer of services. This

---

- Self-employed but still within the scope of a parent organization and paid a retainer to work on a contract basis.
- Employed by an organization to work at home full-time, as in one company where 70 per cent of the workforce operate this arrangement; this trend is increasing.
- Part-time employment with a company, fully at home.
- Employed to work partly at home.
- Dividing work between home base and a telecottage, either self-employed or linked to an organization.
- Employed by more than one company and working at home.

Figure 6.1 Categories of home-working

may involve quite significant learning needs. All boss–employee relationships have this aspect of buyer and seller but, within organizations, this is normally an unspoken relationship; in the case of home-working the relationship must be out in the open.

The scope for home-working is considerable and the development of technology will make it even more viable. For example, a teacher of music can contact a number of classrooms at one time through the use of an electronic whiteboard; what is written in the home appears almost instantly in the classrooms and with the use of teleconferencing a network is complete. The development of local area networks (LANs) linked to computer workstations, with laser printer, full electronic mail capacity, electronic filing, graphics and text production of desk-top publishing quality, will revolutionize most jobs concerned with information. Much discussion currently concerns whether only certain people are 'suitable' for this kind of working. Must we therefore assume that those who are 'unsuitable' are also untrainable? One mistake seems to be that learning needs for such work emphasize only the mechanics of handling the equipment. Little attention appears to have been given as to how people can be supported in order to come to terms with the less tangible aspects of home-working. There can be feelings of isolation, feelings of inadequacy when faced with meeting work demands without the close support of others, or feeling that skills and knowledge are not being updated due to being away from the central activities. It is these aspects of work practices that cause some senior managers to say rather grandly 'Oh you have to be the right personality type to handle this working arrangement.' Use of a strategy for the analysis of all learning needs could lead to a comprehensive programme of support for home-workers. This support ought to be provided by those organizations that are planning to move employees out into the home, whether as self-employed on contract basis or as fully employed home-workers.

For people who plan to work in this way independently, excellent advice and learning material regarding the financial aspects are available from banks such as Barclays, but little comparable learning support is provided to cover the equally important but less tangible aspects of working from home. One stumbling block seems to be the difficulty in analysing exactly where the learning needs lie.

When the force field technique is used in connection with home-working, a principal driving force is the cost of overheads to a company. For facilities in London this has been estimated at around 35 per cent of business costs. Another driving force is the technological imperative; new technology is available and is developing so it must be used. Home-working is one way to utilize these developments to the full. A further significant driving force is that productivity is much higher among home-workers; most organizations have sophisticated in-built time-wasting mechanisms. On the other hand there are restraining forces, and it is among these that a number of the clues to learning needs exist. The feeling of isolation is probably the strongest of these restraining forces and learning to overcome this feeling through various types of support is a priority for any training programme in this area. The problem of intruding upon domestic life is another force where learning how to handle home-working relationships becomes vital. An identity problem is also apparent among people who previously identified themselves largely through their corporate workplace and the various relationships that took place there. Again this reveals a learning need. There is a need to learn how to identify more fully with projects and tasks, and with the new role as being dominant, rather than with features of an organization. The cartoon storyboard is a very useful way of building up a new identity away from any corporate images.

Summary

The main purpose of this chapter has been to set the scene by describing typical changes to working patterns. In each example it has been possible to recognize implications for the way that people use knowledge and practise their skills. Before any techniques can be used to analyse these changing patterns of work, some understanding is required about the kinds of knowledge and skill that are being subjected to change, in some cases quite radical change. This is the subject of the following two chapters.

7   Investigating motor skills

Self-diagnosis

Begin this diagnostic section by thinking of one precise physical task that you do or you are familiar with that is highly skilled, then think of a second physical task that is skilled and a third that is a low level skill. Next examine which elements of these three tasks make them different and in particular, what makes the first more skilled than the second, and the second task more skilled than the third. Anyone who seeks to assess learning needs should be able to assess differences between skilled tasks in this way. In this chapter we will examine these differences as they apply to motor skills, but it is a good idea to see how far you can describe skilled behaviour on the basis of your current knowledge.

Another diagnostic question for you is whether all single skilled movements we make are equally skilled. This may seem a strange question at first but just imagine that in every example of physical movement that we can think of, there are no other elements involved. What is meant by this is that many motor movements we call skilled also involve perceptual skill and/or cognitive skill as an integrated part of our skilled behaviour. If you think simply of the physical movements on their own, are any more skilled than others? To help demonstrate what is meant by single skilled movement, consider the physical movements involved in the list of tasks in Figure 7.1 and thinking only of these movements, can you say with some certainty that some are more skilled than others?

Expect there to be some difficulty in detaching yourself from your preconceived ideas about the 'jobs' with which these skilled tasks are asso-

---

- Plastering
- Hairstyling
- Soldering
- Driving
- Tooth-capping

- Welding
- Electronic assembly
- Laying bricks
- Computer mouse operation
- Domestic product assembly

Figure 7.1   Some motor skill tasks

ciated. You will be inclined to say that, of course, tooth-capping is more skilled than assembly, but while this may be the case it is not necessarily so in terms of motor movement. The examination of skilled motor movement in this isolated way, reveals that some of the most basic tasks have within them one or more skilled motor movements that can be difficult for some people to learn. The actual nature of the movement itself requires careful thought. The precise motor movement involved in plastering, for example, can be described as highly skilled and unique in that it does not easily transfer to other tasks. On the other hand soldering, tooth-capping and welding share the critical skill element of timing, that is, being able to judge the amount of time required as a movement is made. It is worth pondering this list for a while and thinking in the way I have described. You will begin to get a feel for what is meant by skilled motor movements.

Looking at the tasks listed in Figure 7.1, identify those which rely also upon integration with perceptual skills, with cognitive skills, or with both. After some practice, the motor movement concerned with product assembly can become automatic, but active conscious perceptual skill is still required to detect any lapses in the quality standard. The same applies to computer mouse operation, except that in this case, it is both motor and perceptual skill that effectively becomes automatic. However, there does appear to be a continued problem here for people who are weak in the abilities of rate control, selective attention, or finger dexterity. Check with the abilities exercise at the end of Chapter 2 (pp. 31–2) to see whether you are able to speculate about which of these abilities are vital to the learning of these motor skill tasks and whether you feel that some of the tasks have a greater number of ability requirements than others. The learning of electronic assembly, and subsequent performance after practice, for example, will be   influenced by arm–hand steadiness, attention to detail, colour discrimination, finger dexterity, information ordering, problem sensitivity, selective attention and visual acuity. If you can imagine someone performing the task of electronic assembly, you should be able to recognize how these particular abilities have an influence on skill learning and performance. Choose one or two tasks from Figure 7.1 and see if you can recognize which abilities may influence learning and performance.

There are a number of factors that can help explain why one motor skill task has greater skill demands than others. At this point you ought to be aware of the difference in the use of the actual physical movement that is quite separate from the use of any other types of skill, the amount of integration with cognitive and/or perceptual skills, and the number of abilities required in order to learn, practise and perform the skilled task. Can you think of other differences that may be used to distinguish one motor task from another?

Finally, think again about the idea that if we knew more about the factors that contribute to the learning of motor skills and could, as a result, improve the learning technology that is available to us, then almost everyone could learn any motor task to the highest possible standard. Is this possible? Is it desirable? What would the implications be for the idea of being less or more intelligent? Despite many attempts by researchers in the field of learning to improve our understanding and improve learning support, there is a strange idea that there must be better and worse performers among people. If learning support were to become so effective that everyone could achieve top results, the most likely reaction would be that the assessment was too easy. In other words, it seems that without a proportion of people failing we cannot recognize success.

What are motor skills?

The term motor skill is used to describe all physical movements that are made in such a way that the human behaviour can be called skilled. Whether the movements require or do not require learning and practice is the basic determinant of being skilled. Picking up a pencil is a motor movement but cannot be said to require any significant learning and practice. Learning is simply defined as a change in behaviour: no more no less. Once we have hold of the pencil and attempt to do something meaningful with it, a change in behaviour is required which will not occur unless learning takes place. All motor skill use involves a period of learning, followed, if necessary, by a period of practice to consolidate the learning and to increase the speed at which the behaviour is performed. This relationship between learning and practice is illustrated in Figure 7.2.

We first learn how to perform motor skills then practice to increase speed, but speed does not normally come through learning. A common mistake when planning for learning need is to attempt to increase speed at the same time that the skilled movement is being learned. It is for this reason, possibly more than any other, that training is generally looked upon as the most appropriate way to learn motor skill.

Training, when correctly performed, allows for each motor skill to be learned in the setting of a job and once the learning of 'how to do' is complete, a guided practice period takes over on the actual job. The guided practice continues to a point where the skills have been adequately reinforced and the necessary speed-related standard has been achieved. This facility for direct job-related learning and practice is a strength of the apprenticeship system that is still encouraged in some industrialized countries. The principle of the apprentice system applies to jobs where cognitive skills predominate such as accountancy, law and teaching but,

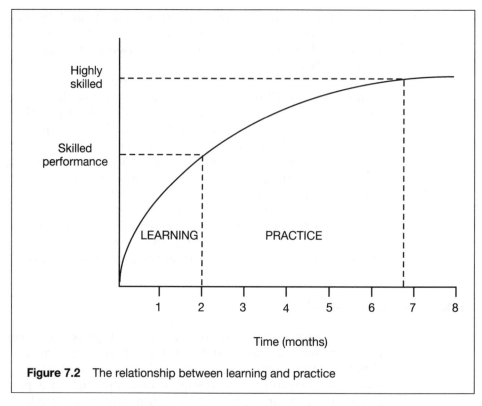

Figure 7.2   The relationship between learning and practice

regrettably, in some countries this form of learning support is now denied to those who wish to learn jobs where motor skills predominate. The principle of apprenticeship was first developed around the learning of motor skills because it was recognized that motor skills need this form of learning support, even if people at the time did not express the need in these words.

There are five recognized types of motor skill movement:

1. Discrete movement
    This involves limb movement which is performed in a very precise and isolated way. Examples can be found among people at power station control panels, during music record making and television programme control.
2. Repetitive movement
    As the name implies, this movement involves repetition of well-learned tasks within short timeframes. Examples of this movement can be found in electronic assembly, packing, and factory-based sewing.
3. Continuous movement
    This movement occurs when the limbs have to maintain a steady movement over a short or prolonged period of time. Examples of this movement can be found in driving, operating a circular saw and fork-lift truck operation.

4. Static steady movement
   This is not really movement, but an essential part of some skilled motor movements; it is the controlled holding of an object in place. Examples can be found in gas welding, hair-styling and threading a needle.
5. Sequential movement
   This movement occurs where one movement is dependent upon the previous movement and also dictates the next movement. Examples can be found in word processing, general typing and product assembly.

Each of the types of motor skill listed above can have different learning requirements. Whenever a task that contains motor skills is being investigated for the analysis of learning needs, we need to know which type of motor skill is involved. Some tasks involve simultaneous use of a combination of these motor skill types: driving combines continuous movement with discrete and sequential movement. One of the most important reasons for knowing about skills at this level of detail is that the wrong approach to identifying needs, and subsequent wrong kind of learning, can lead not only to poor performance, but also to a short shelf-life for the skills. Discrete motor movements, for example, have been shown to have a shorter shelf-life than continuous movements, unless the learning of them is handled correctly. When specifying learning needs for someone who operates control panels, where discrete movement is critical, the learning of each movement should be reinforced by some form of clear feedback to the person who is learning, and practice to establish familiarity and speed should be immediately available following the period of learning. This particular job also involves sequential movement, which also has a short shelf-life, unless the learning is planned with care.

An important requirement in the analysis of learning needs for motor skills is the provision of adequate opportunities for feedback or what is sometimes called knowledge of results (KR). The learning of motor skills is highly dependent upon the feedback received at different stages of the learning process. If we think of learning to drive, the motor skill movements that are involved can be performed quite easily by most people. One hour on a driving simulator would demonstrate that the multi-limb coordination used in changing gear can be mastered without difficulty. The continuous motor skill movement of steering can be grasped in a similar way, so why do people require many hours of tuition before they can drive?

The main problem lies in the use each learner makes of feedback. Feedback in motor skill learning takes a number of forms that are either perceptual or kinaesthetic. The perceptual feedback is based upon how we interpret the various sights and sounds that come back at us after making a skilled motor movement: the tennis player picks up feedback from the sound of contact; the potter gains immediate feedback from the sight of clay being formed. Kinaesthetic feedback comes through muscle spindles that sense the slightest changes in our use of muscles. When some people are particularly sensitive to this form of feedback, we often say they have the 'knack'. It appears that there is still much to be learned about how muscle spindles operate in providing us with feedback; if, as in the case of abilities, we knew more, people could be much more skilled.

In the example of driving, feedback becomes a very complex business. First, the kinaesthetic feedback comes to the driver from the road but only through the body of the car, rather than directly. The perceptual feedback to the learner driver is considerable; one of the key learning needs for the learner is to select and use the various pieces of feedback that are relevant to the task of driving. It is this learning task of selection, plus the driver's response to kinaesthetic feedback, that explains the time-lag between being able to master the motor movements and being sufficiently skilled to pass a test.

Most readers will be able to identify with the role of feedback in learning the skilled task of driving. However, the principle applies to all motor skill learning and whenever it is necessary for a motor skill to be learned, a question must be asked about the feedback that is involved. When the feedback has been identified, the next step is to ask what learning needs exist in order to select and use the necessary feedback effectively; learning to use feedback is a learning need.

Another form of feedback comes from people around the learner: colleagues, an instructor, or a supervisor. If it is to be effective, this type of feedback has to be specific to the task being learned, not the patronizing pat on the back of 'You're doing well'. The personal feedback has to be constructive, such as providing an accurate comparison between the learner's position an hour or a day earlier and the present. Awareness about the most appropriate form that personal feedback should take is an essential ingredient of learning needs support, and should be identified.

Motor skills and ways of working

There has been a distinct shift in the typical use of motor skills as a result of changes in the conduct of working practices. Fifty years ago, to write a list of specific motor skill tasks used in industry and commerce would have been a huge job. The same task is very much easier now, because there has been a sharp decline in the amount of motor skill used and, in particular, a decline in the amount of high level use of this type of skill. The main implication for learning needs of this trend is simply that you ought to be aware that there is a steady movement towards the lessening of motor skill use. We already have examples of this type of skill becoming obsolete such as in the use of manually operated machine tools, newspaper printing, plumbing, shipwrighting, house painting, car manufacture and electronic assembly. All occupations of this kind have witnessed a significant de-skilling and it is in the area of motor skill use that the biggest impact has been felt. In contrast, there are still pockets of activity where motor skill predominates and is likely to continue to do so for some time. Typical examples are hairdressing, welding, bricklaying and plastering, be-spoke carpentry and stonemasonry. With the exceptions of hairdressing, bricklaying and plastering, there are threats to other motor skills from likely developments in technology and it is difficult to imagine how any extensive use of occupational motor skills can be preserved well into the next century.

Despite the general demise in motor skill use, requirements for motor skill may be introduced as part of new technological development. The computer mouse is possibly the best example. It calls for a combination of motor and perceptual skills that some people seem to have difficulty in fully mastering. In this, as in other aspects of learning difficulty, it helps to look at the influence of our abilities. Another combined motor and perceptual skill task that has been created by a new technology is the initial hand control of robots during a programming process. Although this is a task that some people can learn quite quickly, there are others who find the task difficult to learn. In addition to perceptual skill, the motor skill used in this task consists of continuous, discrete, and sequential movements. In investigating this task for the purpose of analysing learning needs, it is necessary to take these types of movement into account as well as to explore the perceptual skill involved in three-dimensional shape recognition.

A number of automated and semi-automated processes now require fine adjustments to be made that introduce a specific example of motor skill use. When planning for learning need in areas of new technology, it is still necessary to question the possibility of motor skill requirements. If not, quite subtle and unexpected motor skill requirements can emerge. The result is often that people become involved who have been trained in all other aspects of the technology, except that one area where some people are not trainable. The control of complex printing or chemical processes from remote display panels relies a good deal upon the ability of visualization; the operator must be able to transfer panel images to real events that cannot be immediately observed. Some people find this difficult to do, and quite sophisticated learning support is required to overcome learning difficulties in this area. Even then, visualization can be quite resistant to any form of learning support.

Another important aspect of motor skill that has been affected by changes to working practices is the shelf-life of this type of skill. The idea that a skill has a shelf-life is not commonly recognized but most of the evidence about how well skill remains with us is anecdotal. When the question of shelf-life is raised, the most common reply concerns reference to skills such as bicycle riding or shoelace tying; remember how difficult it was to learn this last motor skill? Some motor skills do remain after quite long periods of inaction but the indications are that motor skills associated with new technology can easily be lost. This applies especially where the skill involves discrete movement combined with perceptual and/or cognitive skills, and when there is no immediate reinforcement and practice after initial learning.

An example of motor skill shelf-life can be seen in the use of computer numerical control (CNC) machine tools. Particularly during the 1970s and

1980s when organizations invested heavily in this technology, it was common for skilled centre-lathe turners to attend courses delivered by the manufacturers of the machines. The purpose of these training courses was to help people learn the skills of programming and operation of the machines. In some cases the training programme was arranged in advance of the machine installation resulting in a time-lapse between the end of the course and the delivery of the machines. The outcome was that course members lost the newly acquired skills and in some cases it was as though they had not even attended a training course. This problem has been observed more recently in the case of learning diagnostic and setting methods for the latest electronics application on newspaper printing presses. When people do not have the opportunity to use what are combined motor, perceptual and cognitive skills, the lack of early re-inforcement leads to a short shelf-life for the skills. There is also the possibility that skills associated with new technology can be lost even after a period of reinforcement through practice.

The implications of shelf-life for the analysis of learning needs are to be found mainly in the timing of learning support and whether, despite the existence of a need, there may be difficulty in sustaining the skill once it has been acquired. To make this point clear it is worth noting the tendency to train for skills rather than to train for jobs. The term, 'skills for the future' is, in fact, a misnomer; it should be 'effective learning for the future'.

Some skills can be stockpiled, and learning these skills can be of value in the long term, but many current skills cannot be stored in this way. Even some so-called core skills, which by definition should persist through the practice of a particular job, can be lost over time. The problem becomes acute when unemployed people are helped to identify learning needs in order to find suitable placement on a training course. With the best of intentions, on the part of the organizers, the aim is to provide such people with skills so that they may find suitable work. What is normally lacking in such needs assessment is the knowledge that the respective skills are dependent upon sound reinforcement and continued practice in order to sustain them in a usable form. Where a skill will be lost without such re-inforcement there is a strong argument for training only when a job follow-up can be assured. Thus the need becomes one of training for jobs instead of training for skills that cannot be sustained. These are vital issues for people who are charged with analysing learning needs in the present volatile job market.

Investigating a motor skill

The previous discussion has been theoretical, but an example of motor skill investigation and the consequent learning needs analysis will now be presented.

The example concerns an area of skill not yet discussed in this book – hand glass-making. New technology has yet to have significant impact in this area, although the use of robotics appears to be a possibility for the future.

The first part of the investigation was to determine, by skills analysis, the types of skill being used. Motor skills were clearly used in handling the rods of molten glass, in blowing the glass and in the complex forming of glass into shape by hand. Less obvious perceptual skills were involved in the recognition of colour, shape and sensing by touch when forming glass into the shape of a mould. It was then necessary to look for particular features of these two types of skill. One that was quite important concerned the use of both hands simultaneously; this was a clear example of continuous movement which once mastered would remain with the person.

When a skill involves combined use of two hands, the right-hand–left-hand debate may arise. At quite an early age people who are naturally left-handed are more dextrous with their non-preferred hand than are right-handed people with their non-preferred left hand. Generally speaking left-handed people can be expected to be more skilled in two-handed use than right-handed people. Right-handed people are more likely to be preferred-hand dominant. Despite this, it is usual for glass factories to be designed so strongly towards right-handed movements, that left-handed people, who ought to have the strongest potential for this skill, can be disadvantaged. This right-handed bias also applies to areas of new technology such as computer workstation operation and point-of-sale terminal use in retail stores.

In glass-making, two-handed dexterity applies to the turning of a rod bearing the molten glass while in a mould and to the turning of a rod with one hand while the other hand forms glass into a required shape. The two-handed operation can be extended to multi-limb operation with a mould operated by foot while still handling the rod of molten glass. This detailed examination of skill use was gathered using the critical incident technique with four highly skilled glassmakers who produced reproduction and novel glassware. The particular learning difficulties were explored by using the same technique with two trainees.

The perceptual skills of this work also have particular features. One important feature is the sensing of touch when the glass is reaching a formed state in a mould. There is also the perception of a correct pick-up of glass from the furnace and a recognition of colour state. The further investigation of such skills can be facilitated by the identification of abilities that are critical to the learning of these skills. The ability requirement in this case matches quite closely that of welding. It is quite possible therefore that skilled people in these two areas of work could exchange jobs, with confidence that the skills could be learned quite quickly.

Of the thirty abilities described in Chapter 2, nine are directly related to motor skills and seven to perceptual skills. These are listed in Figure 7.3. Glass-making of this kind involves a high proportion of these perceptual–motor abilities, which is one indication of the task complexity. The ability requirements for the skilled glassmaker are body orienta-

---

Motor skill related abilities
Hand–arm steadiness
Body orientation
Dynamic strength
Finger dexterity
Flexibility of movement
Manual dexterity
Multi-limb coordination
Rate control
Static strength

Perceptual skill related abilities
Colour discrimination
General hearing
Perceptual speed
Selective attention
Speed of focusing
Visual acuity
Visualization

Figure 7.3   Motor skill and perceptual skill abilities

---

tion, visualization, colour discrimination, rate control, finger dexterity, manual dexterity, multi-limb coordination, visual acuity, and hand–arm steadiness.

If glassmakers were asked to describe the learning requirement of what is basically a motor skill, it is unlikely that they would offer this level of detail. Similarly it is difficult for them to explain why so many years of experience are required to reach a highly skilled level of performance. The traditional method of learning the skill is through training by part-learning, that is, working gradually from simple tasks to ever-increasing complexity. It is this practice that is called experience and is the accepted way of learning.

Effective analysis of learning needs demands that such accepted ways should be questioned no matter how uncomfortable this may be. One of the main approaches to challenging current training habits is to investigate the whole process that surrounds the skill use. Introducing technology in one part of a process often makes certain practices obsolete but there remains a belief that the need still exists. Another approach is to take account of the learning technology that is available to support a new method of learning. For our glassmakers, the introduction of simulation techniques or multi-media use can speed up skill learning in such a way that the identified needs also change. In practice, simulation in the form of a jig to allow for a recording of the rod turning speed provides the learner with immediate feedback. This accelerates learning replacing lengthy learning by trial and error, while multi-media use can provide ready learning feedback for colour recognition and shape forming. Therefore, knowledge of the latest learning support available is an important part of any learning needs analysis; needs cannot be divorced from the means available for their satisfaction.

What can be learned from the example?

The traditional approach to training needs analysis for hand glass-making stresses the obvious motor skills of glass-handling, glass-blowing and glass-forming, and the knowledge that is required to support these skills. However, a lack of insight into the actual process of learning is apparent and consequently it is accepted that most skill acquisition is gained through experience. The analysis of glass-making provides, in outline, a sequence of investigation that allows for a deeper understanding of the skilled process. Three techniques were applied: structured observation, critical incident and the abilities approach. The technique of structured observation is particularly suited to motor skills of this kind, and the use of critical incidents helps to tease out the information about the less obvious perceptual skills and also allows for an exploration of incidents where motor and perceptual skills are used in tandem.

In traditional work areas such as glass-making, resistance tends to be shown towards any methods that can shorten skill learning time. It is understandable that where learning time is a factor that contributes to the status of a skill, any attempt to reduce that time will be met with resistance if not hostility. The lesson to be gained is that when analysing learning needs a basic question needs to be asked: 'Is the need to satisfy the learning of existing skills or does the need also include the possible improvement of existing skill learning and subsequent use?' Learning for improvement is very different from learning new skills and knowledge. In the case described here the aim was to identify learning needs that could lead to improved performance. One of the main obstacles to such an investigation is that skilled people believe that their traditional practices are being questioned and their initial reservation has to be overcome. A further obstacle is the realization that although clear needs can be identified for the purpose of performance improvement, the means of providing the necessary support may not be there, and motivation to satisfy the needs may be lacking among those people who are vital to the whole process.

The two techniques of critical incident and listening and questioning are particularly valuable in the collection of information about motor skill use. An investigator who is skilled in the use of both techniques can gather a considerable body of descriptive information about a motor skill; an almost totally exhaustive description will be gained from no more than six skilled practitioners, whatever the skill under investigation. Listening and questioning will allow you to focus attention quite specifically, while the critical incident technique can cover all areas of a skill's use. A follow-up with protocol analysis and/or skills analysis will provide considerable insight into what has to be learned in order to become fully skilled. The abilities approach is especially helpful in showing how well people can be expected to transfer from an 'old' motor skill to the 'new' one being investigated. It provides a basis for comparison with other skills and can help explain the reasons for particular difficulties in learning.

Summary

Although motor skills are in decline in industrialized countries, there are still pockets of industrial activity where such skills are very important. People working in these industries, who are responsible for analysing learning needs, should review learning methods from time to time. As pointed out in the self-diagnosis section at the beginning of the chapter, it is helpful to have a 'feel' for what is involved in the learning of motor skills. Such awareness makes it easier to respond to the learning needs that can arise from changing motor skill use. It is a good idea at this stage to reflect upon the ideas you had when reading the self-diagnosis section, to see whether there has been any enhanced awareness on your part.

8 Investigating perceptual and thinking skills

Self-diagnosis

We make sense of things around us by interpreting what we see and what is gathered from our other senses. We call this perceptual skill and it involves far more than what we see. Making use of our perceptual skills involves interpreting the various messages we get from our senses and our reactions are likely to occur soon after the message has been received. Often, these messages are processed by what we call thinking; any message of interest is compared with information already held in our memory and out comes a result. It is how this 'thinking' process is carried out that we call cognitive skill. Many different behaviours can be recognized as examples of either cognitive or perceptual skills.

Some jobs have a strong bias towards cognitive skills, towards perceptual skills or maintain an even balance between the two. When you think about skills in this way it soon becomes apparent that for some tasks it is necessary to use both types of skill simultaneously, perhaps with the addition of a motor skill. If you believe that new learning needs have emerged as a result of changing practices, it helps to know the existing mix of skills and the new mix that will be needed as a result of the changes.

Think about a current job, or one that you are familiar with, and identify the mix of skills in this way.

Given that the use of cognitive skills is based upon how we process information in the brain, any investigation of what makes someone skilled in this area is likely to be difficult. However, we cannot truly analyse learning needs unless we know what actually contributes to effective performance in a given task.

Can you name at least two techniques, either from those listed in Figure 1.1 in the first chapter (p. 5), or from your own experience, that would be suitable for investigating how someone performs a cognitive skill task?

Similar difficulties are experienced when investigating perceptual skills. If the skill was based entirely upon what people see around them, then there would be few problems because we would all see the same. If you do not agree with the last statement, then consider what are the main issues that make you question it. Given equal levels of hearing, two people will hear the same sounds, but due to different levels of listening skill they will often record information as though they had heard different sounds. In the same way, it can be argued that we do see the same things around us but it is perceptual skill that dictates how the visions are recorded and interpreted.

Can you think of at least two techniques that are suitable for the investigation of perceptual skills?

There is a shift from motor skills to cognitive and perceptual skills, as a result of changing technology – do you feel that this trend will continue and that in perhaps twenty years from now there will be very few occupational tasks that make use of motor skill? If you do feel that the trend will continue, what are the wider implications for analysing learning needs? If you think that there could be a return to motor skill use, how realistic is it that some of the skills could be lost and become extinct during the intervening period? When thinking about this question, you may like to reflect upon what has been said in this book about the idea of a shelf-life for skills.

Training needs analysis often arises from the fact that something has gone wrong, and is often detected from symptoms such as poor customer reactions, falling sales, falling production, or lack of new ideas. Many of these symptoms can indicate a misuse of cognitive or perceptual skills, or a lack of these skills. This approach to analysing needs, while quite valid, can be seen as negative and, at times, reactive. An alternative is to base learning needs upon what it is that the most effective people do well, that is, adopt a positive as opposed to a negative approach to the subject. This requires a change in perception of how we improve performance. A useful analogy comes from engineering-based manufacture, where it is common to talk in negative terms of machine down time. This is measured in the number of hours of lost production due to faults, material problems, lack of skills or poor scheduling. When the negative approach to learning needs is adopted, it is often the amount of down time that prompts a call for new or better learning; 'training' needs are often recognized as an important element in attempts to reduce down time. On the other hand some companies talk about up time and seek ways, including 'training' needs, to improve this up time.

Some people might say that to make this distinction is only playing with words, but it is only through our use of words that we can exercise our cognitive and perceptual skill. Even when words are not spoken, they are used to internalize our thoughts. A change in wording does not necessarily change our perception; it is our change in perception that causes us to change how we describe something. The changed perception in the engineering example means that a positive approach to the analysis of learning needs leads to an investigation of what the most effective people do to achieve high up time. In contrast, the negative approach leads to avoidance-learning and less opportunity is available to exploit 'best practice'. Another aspect of word use in this sense, is that the positive approach can reflect a perception of working behaviour as being effective, appropriate, efficient and fair, as opposed to being problem-oriented. The difference between taking a positive or negative approach to the analysis of learning needs serves as an example of perception. If you have experience of training needs analysis (TNA), has this process been prompted partly by examples of negative behaviour or of positive behaviour?

Perception and thinking

The study of perception and cognition has kept researchers busy since the time of the early Greeks and the activity shows little sign of slowing down. It is interesting to speculate on the reactions of early Greek philosophers if they had the opportunity to experience life today. Surprise and wonder at all the new artifacts of life, such as computers, rockets and television, would be inevitable, and they would also feel somewhat out of their depth. In sharp contrast, however, they would feel perfectly at ease when discussing the processes that make human beings behave in the way they do. One reaction from the Greeks might well be, 'Haven't you found an explanation for these behaviours yet?' Each new finding simply prompts further questions for exploration.

Some progress has been made over the past 2000 years, that can help us have more insight into the use of cognitive and perceptual skills and some of the findings can aid the analysis of our learning needs. Most of the progress in this area has resulted in us becoming more aware of the typical needs to be fulfilled if people are to be more effective in the use of the skills.

An experiment by Asch (1956) has made us aware that our use of perceptual skill can be influenced by others. A group of people were shown a diagram of three vertical lines, labelled A, B and C, of which two, A and C, were clearly of the same length. The identification of which lines matched was a very basic perceptual task. All but one person in the group had been told previously to say that A and B matched; these people were collaborators in the experiment. Repeated tests showed that the solitary person was unlikely to contradict the decision of the group, even though it was obviously wrong. The experiment was extended to a solitary, non-collaborating, person who was in a waiting room when smoke began to appear. The immediate reaction of the person was to leave the room to report the smoke. This experiment was repeated a number of times with the same result. Then the experiment was conducted with a number of collaborators in the waiting room who were told not to react to the smoke. The most common result was that the solitary non-collaborating person also remained seated. A more disturbing experiment was conducted in which the solitary person in the waiting room heard someone scream outside, and again the reaction each time was for the person to investigate what was happening outside the room. However, when a number of collaborators were told to ignore the scream, the reaction of the solitary person was most often to remain seated. On this evidence, it may increase your chances of being helped when mugged if only one person is on hand rather than a crowd.

That we are influenced in our actions by being in groups or teams is important knowledge when planning for learning needs. The findings about influence upon perception are relevant to our learning about team-working, in particular for project teams or for taking decisions in meetings. Although we are still some way from providing explanations for this type of behaviour, an awareness that it exists can be of value to those who analyse learning needs.

A current trend is to give people more say and responsibility in how they conduct their working practices. Some people use the term 'empowerment' as though a new process had been discovered, even though the process has been in use in many companies for over a hundred years. It can be difficult to analyse the needs of people who are required to work in an autonomous way; although we tend to value freedom and independence, humans are essentially social animals and only a relatively small percentage is happy with real independence of action. It can be argued that the attempt to increase this small percentage, whether desirable or not, is a demanding task that requires a high level of understanding about how people behave at work. Whether people accept or do not accept moves to give them greater autonomy is a result of the way they exercise their cognitive and perceptual skills. Before we can analyse the needs of people who are asked to accept greater responsibility, we need to know something about how they perceive and rationalize their current working situation. We must recognize that people apply their perceptual skills differently to the same circumstances and some people do not necessarily perceive greater responsibility and autonomy as a 'good' thing. Thus, it is understandable if such people do not take kindly to being told that, in order to exploit their new-found freedom and responsibility, they have learning needs.

The issues of group behaviour, autonomy and organizational structure, in relation to perception and cognition will now be explored further.

Identification of cognitive skills

The well-documented increase in the use of cognitive skills at work as a proportion of other skills, justifies our attempts to arrive at a strategy that can help us analyse learning needs that arise from the use of these skills. In the past it was common for the word 'skill' to be used only in relation to manual or motor tasks. In many cases a skilled person performed manual tasks in an automatic way as a result of many years of practice; now much skilled work does not remain the same long enough for these years of practice to be accumulated. We can no longer rely upon a slow process of experience gathering. Learning needs are now dynamic, mainly because of the stronger emphasis upon thinking and, in particular, the different types of problem-solving that are required.

So, how can we best describe these cognitive skills? One way that helps us understand the skills is to use the analogy of a computer. In trying to make computer-controlled machines behave as humans behave, there is a spin-off in coming to a better understanding of how humans actually behave. If we want to know how a computer produces results after the processing of information that has been entered, it is more helpful to investigate the software that is in use rather than the machine itself. Human beings are little different in this respect; we have our 'machine' parts of the brain but we also have our own unique programs for processing information. When teachers discuss the topic of 'learning to learn' it is largely the improvement of these programs that is being talked about. When we think about cognitive skills, it becomes apparent that some people have more effective programs than others, that is, they can process information at faster speeds or can handle complex conceptual ideas more readily. These people we tend to describe as being more 'intelligent' and in a society where cognitive skill is more highly valued than other skills, this title of 'intelligent' is desirable. An important question concerning the analysis of learning needs in this area is, 'What do people need in order to make their programs meet the requirements of any job they wish to do?' As with computer programs there can be 'bugs' in our own programs, which provide blocks to learning (Downs 1992), and freeing such blocks is of interest to those who analyse learning needs.

There is no 'magic' way to tap into a generally effective human program; as with the computer there are appropriate programs for particular sets of tasks. Despite the claims of some people that there is a 'general intelligence', it is quite difficult to justify such a statement. It could be assumed that the only factor which prevents us from learning anything to the highest possible standard, is our lack of understanding about how our programs for dealing with cognitive skills work.

To recognize cognitive skill needs we need to investigate the behaviours of people who are most skilled in a particular context and then compare their skilled behaviours with the behaviour of people who want to perform the skill. Such an investigation commonly occurs when a new process is being introduced for the first time, as in the transfer to new print technology in the newspaper industry, in the introduction of new point-of-sale terminals in large retail businesses and in the move by some companies to financial accountability at lower levels of the organization. In these and other similar examples of new technology and new working practices, cognitive skill needs are difficult to describe and consequently difficult to support. Usually at least one person has some mastery of the technology, either within the supplying firm, within a parent or sister company, or a service technician. Another question concerns any special requirements that may arise from the use of the technology or new practice in a particular setting. There then has to be reliance upon some controlled discovery learning before clear learning needs can be analysed.

When analysing cognitive skill need, it is not always possible to find explicit instructions; there are times when it is necessary to allow for exploration and discovery learning to take place. If you have had contact with young children, you may like to reflect upon how much they are capable of learning without the aid of clear instructions; they appear to be skilled in using exploration and discovery, which seems to diminish as many of us grow older. When faced with the need to learn new skills and knowledge as opposed to learn for 'improvement', the opportunity to explore puts people in a better position to ask meaningful questions. For some people who are not computer literate, there can be considerable difficulty in asking meaningful questions when faced with a specialist who is there to 'help' them. If, for example, they are allowed to explore a system in use, the discovered knowledge can lead to questions that, in turn, can assist the specialist in identifying further learning needs.

For the analysis of cognitive skill need, there is a limited number of techniques available. An appropriate choice of techniques can be made from protocol analysis, critical incident and the abilities requirement approach. These techniques are the most productive and effective. A specialist or highly skilled person can provide considerable insight into how cognitive processing is carried out during the performance of a skilled task. The choice of critical incident or protocol analysis is largely determined by the person giving the skill information. Protocol analysis relies upon a person being particularly articulate; in ability requirement terms, this amounts to a combination of word fluency, information ordering and idea fluency. In the case of an 'expert' who has difficulty in articulating the skilled behaviours it is more advisable to use the critical incident technique, because the technique has been designed to overcome this kind of difficulty.

In following an investigation of this kind the 'experts' will often begin to reflect upon their own experience of learning the skill and will emphasize particular features where people who need to learn may require special attention. In this sense it is of value if one or more people can be found who have experience of teaching the skill. In this case of learning about how people learn, the technique of critical incident is probably the most effective.

Cognitive skill has so far been discussed in general terms, but we will now examine some practical examples of cognitive skill use at work.

Examples of cognitive skill use

A retail salesperson giving change

There are a number of ways to perform the task of giving change. Some people have developed more effective programs for processing this information, as different lengths of queues at some retail outlets will testify. In some cases, such as cake shops, long queues are desirable but in most places they are bad for business. In the case of advanced point-of-sale operation, where the problem of calculating change has been removed, there can be an added dimension of motor skill movement. Long queues, using the negative approach to the analysis of learning needs, can be a symptom that a need of this kind exists.

A similar example of this type of cognitive skill comes from a firm that operated in an area where piece-work was standard practice, and where young people grew up listening to their parents talk about the calculation of their rates. When the firm opened a new factory in an area that had been traditionally dominated by heavy industry and where little piece-work was used, the management encountered problems. Despite the more up-to-date machinery at the new site, production was significantly lower in comparison with the parent company. Consultants discovered that the reason was the time being spent adding up totals of units made, because a number of the young people leaving school did not have the cognitive skill of multiplication. In the other area family working traditions had compensated for the lack of this skill and learning took place outside school. Given that people do have the necessary basic numeracy there is still a requirement, in some jobs, to identify what needs to be learned in order to have an effective program for tasks of this kind.

A police officer investigating a domestic burglary

The investigation of a domestic burglary involves a complex set of cognitive skills, which is further complicated by the need to use well-developed perceptual skills when responding appropriately to the house occupants. The main cognitive skill involves the processing of information, by comparing what the house occupants say with information about similar incidents, in an attempt to build up a profile of likely criminals. Some police approaches to this task are found to be effective and pleasing to the public concerned, but there are examples of approaches by police officers that are not welcomed. The learning needs of officers who displease members of the public have to be analysed and the technique of critical incident has been used to good effect with victims of burglary.

People were able to provide numerous critical incidents of police officer behaviour that either pleased or displeased. Interestingly, it was the incidents about what 'pleased' the victims which provided the most effective information for the analysis of learning needs, and identified what ought to be included in subsequent training programmes. This is a further example of a positive approach to the identification of learning needs, as opposed to an approach that emphasizes problems.

A bank manager deciding upon a loan application

A judgement of this kind involves the use of cognitive skills in conjunction with perceptual skills. An important question to be asked is whether managers use their perceptual skills first in forming an opinion about loan worthiness, or whether they wait until cognitive skill has been used in processing the relevant information before making an important decision.

Almost inevitably an impression based upon perception is formed first and this tends to influence the subsequent processing of information. Where it can be identified that the most effective loan-making decisions are made by separating out the use of the two different types of skill, then how this is achieved becomes a learning need for managers who have less impressive loan-making records. What is possibly a little explored area is the eventual success of businesses that have been refused support by particular managers; what cognitive processes took place to allow such profitable businesses to escape the bank?

Techniques that are appropriate in this case can be narrowed down to protocol analysis and critical incident, and preferably both are used to gather detailed information that leads to the analysis of learning needs. Broader organizational issues relevant to a bank should be taken into account when making this kind of decision. How information about such issues is processed by respective managers can be usefully tapped by using the delphi technique with a small group of four to six managers who are particularly skilled in loan decision-making. The final report from such a delphi exercise can provide a strong base for the analysis of learning needs in the bank.

The now common competency or 'can-do' statements are of little value in the circumstances typically met by police officers or bank managers, because outcome-related measures are unable to take account of novel events, which they quite frequently encounter. Also, when the same outcome can be arrived at by different approaches, it is the underlying strategy that best reflects effective performance rather than the outcome itself. Only by collecting incidents of most and least effective behaviour is it possible to recognize a most effective use of cognitive skills, in such a way that learning needs can be recognized in others.

A doctor making treatment decisions at the site of a mountain rescue

This example provides a less obvious use of cognitive skills but it is valuable nevertheless. In these circumstances choices have to be made about how strictly rationed expert help is best utilized, because in most cases the services of only one doctor are available. The dilemma is that the climber who appears outwardly to be the most seriously injured may actually be in a less life-threatening state than another climber who has much less outward sign of injury. What additional learning needs exist for a medical doctor who will encounter such incidents? What makes up the program that allows for the most effective use of cognitive skills in this area? Answers to these and other questions are normally looked for among doctors who have amassed a number of such incidents and who can talk through the mental reasoning that takes place. In practice the tendency is for doctors new to this area, who are often climbers themselves, to indulge in discovery learning; eventually the particular skills used in each situation become unique to them. However, a case can be made for the formal recognition of learning needs in this area of work. Critical incident technique and AET would be of particular value.

A newspaper publishing operator's rapid decision-making

The term 'publishing' in newspaper production refers to the sorting and bundling of papers ready for dispatch to wholesalers and retailers. Before the introduction of the microprocessor these tasks were all of the motor skill type. Now the process is controlled by complex semi-automated to fully automated equipment and at times includes the inserting of advertising copy into the newspaper itself. The publishing operator has exchanged motor skills for perceptual and cognitive skills. An important task is to respond quickly to emergency situations when the complex system of machines and conveyors develops faults. First, the operator must have the perceptual skill to recognize what effective operation of the equipment looks like. Without this skill the operator would be unable to anticipate problems and would have to rely upon reactive behaviour when the eventual big problem occurred. Even with high levels of perceptual skills that come mainly through effective vigilance, serious problems can occur and action has to be swift and correct first time. There is often a choice of actions to be taken and it is the person with the most effective cognitive skill program for this task who will respond most quickly and most appropriately. In some cases, operators have been known to ignore warning signs deliberately, or even to ignore serious problems because they lack the confidence to take appropriate action.

In complex processes such as this the two techniques of simulation and protocol analysis probably provide the most effective means of investigating learning needs. The simulation can consist of costly investment in multi-media based computer reproduction of the complex system, or a less costly representation of the system by using multiple overlays on an overhead projector. Another approach is to use a physical model of the plant or system if one already exists, or a three-dimensional drawing. The protocol analysis can then be based upon the chosen method of simulation. The most effective operators talk through their perception of effective working, before moving to the simulation of particular problem events. For each fault event, the operator is asked to talk through the reasoning that was used to arrive at the eventual correct decision. When a number of events have been explored a series of protocols will be revealed, that together indicate the use of a strategy, in other words, a close model of the operator's program. It is unlikely that operators in such situations will have been taught an effective strategy; they will have developed it over time as a result of trial-and-error learning. Three or four such operators ought to provide evidence of strategy use, regardless of whether they arrive at the same correct decisions by the same method of reasoning, and whether more than one effective thinking strategy is at work. However, some operators do not develop such effective strategies and thus a learning need exists as a result. In this case the need will have been derived from most effective behaviour rather than from what the less effective operators do wrong.

Inevitably, such detailed investigation of skill use leads not only to the possible analysis of learning needs, but the in-depth descriptions of what happens at particular incidents also provide valuable information for the development of a learning programme.

Perceptual skill

The previous section has shown that it is not always easy to separate perceptual skill use from that of cognitive skill, or indeed from motor skill. One exercise (Bloomer 1976) helps illustrate how perception and cognition can work together in an almost automatic way suggesting that, at times, we have little control over our reactions.

The exercise consists of collecting a number of cartoons that you find particularly funny, then cutting off the captions from each one. The cartoons are put face down in one pile, the captions in another pile. The cartoons and captions are thoroughly mixed up and are then paired off, still facing down. When each pair of cartoon and caption is turned over at least half will still be seen as funny. In this case our perception of what is called funny is linked with how we process the different bits of information from the picture and from the caption, and it appears from the randomness of this exercise that there may not be much control over this process.

The task of separating cognitive and perceptual skill can be difficult but if you live by the maxim, 'If something is not difficult it is not worth doing', then you will not see this as a problem. Investigation, which is what this book is primarily about, inevitably leads to confrontation with difficulties, but they ought to be welcomed rather than avoided.

Perceptual skill is possibly best recognized as a level of awareness. Some people seem to be acutely aware of their surroundings and sensitive to the smallest changes. Although perception is most commonly associated with sight it includes all that we can absorb from our other senses. The case of a person who regained sight at the age of 51 after losing it when aged 10 months (Gregory 1966) helps illustrate this point. When this once-blind person saw a lathe for the first time, he could not recognize the machine even though he knew how it worked, but when he felt the machine with his eyes closed, he stood back and said, 'Now that I have felt it I can see it'. In this case, as with sighted people, perception is sometimes only complete when more than one sense has been utilized.

Before the introduction of the microprocessor, telephone engineers used four senses in the detection of faults on the switching equipment and their perceptual skill use was very high. The engineers smelt for signs of excess friction, felt for changes in temperature or excess movement, listened for signs of wear and looked for changes in operation. The whole inspection exercise amounted to either effective perception of the switching mechanism or less effective perception and those engineers with less effective perception could often be involved in costly repeat call-backs to fix faults. Now this system has changed with the introduction of the microprocessor and very little inspection is required. When faults occur there is a high demand upon cognitive skill; perceptual skill is now of very limited value, and motor skill, which was crucial to the old practices, is virtually obsolete because the changing of faulted units or modules is quite routine. In this situation the investigation of learning needs leads to the conclusion that it is the cognitive processes of diagnosis and problem-solving that require the greatest attention, and perceptual skill can be separated out and largely ignored. In contrast, the use of perceptual skills in other areas of work has steadily grown. One of the main driving forces for this growth has been the move towards the production of high value goods, particularly in the fashion business.

The experiments, referred to earlier, that show how our perception of situations can be dictated by others are similar to various exercises designed to demonstrate how unreliable our use of perception can be. It is quite difficult for any of us to be sure that what we perceive is 'fact'. In jobs where perceptual skills play a significant role it is worthwhile to check how consistently the skills are being performed.

Here is an exercise for you to try that concerns perception:

FINISHED FILES ARE THE RESULT OF YEARS OF SCIENTIFIC STUDY COMBINED WITH THE EXPERIENCE OF MANY YEARS.

How many Fs can you count?

When you have done this exercise, compare your result with the answer given at the end of this chapter (p. 113).

In Chapter 4 the point was made that hearing is a natural ability, but listening is a skill to be developed. Similarly, we read the words in the exercise, but when asked to use the skill of looking (finding Fs) the results can be quite different between people. In tasks where looking for acute detail is required, such as electronics inspection, instrument panel control and operating theatre nursing, this difference between ability and skill use needs to be taken into account. An important point to be aware of is that our perceptions can be unreliable.

This lack of reliability is made more acute because we feel that what we see is obvious to all and this also applies to our other senses. In this respect there can be a problem in trying to analyse learning needs from the basis of what is going wrong. For example, much time and expense can be spent on training-based solutions to problems where people will inevitably make perceptual errors, irrespective of whether training has been provided. Very often, errors in the use of perceptual skill can only be avoided by changing the way work is organized, or the way that equipment is designed. It has been estimated that about four hundred aircraft were lost during the Second World War due to pilot error. Analysis has shown that the main cause of these errors lay in the design of instrument display which in turn led to errors in the use of perceptual skills (Fitts and Jones 1947).

Although the losses happened fifty years ago, the principle of designing-out faults and error-inducing behaviour still applies strongly today. It can be argued that the phenomenon of 'sick building syndrome' involves perception as well as physical causes. Perceptions of working conditions that arise from being unable to find a piece of wood to touch in the office, of being unable to open a window when you feel like it, or of being over-looked by many others in an open plan office can all contribute to repeated sickness.

There is a strong case for taking a wide view of learning needs; we all need to learn about what people perceive to be human working conditions. It is worth repeating that there is no difference between organizational needs and individual needs, as practised in earlier training needs analysis; there are only needs of people, who together form organizations.

Perceptual skill use is a feature of all jobs but clearly it is more important in some jobs than in others. Proof-reading and airport check-in are extreme examples of use of perceptual skills. Solicitors, unless their learning needs have been adequately covered in this respect, can be adversely influenced by the initial perception they form of their clients. Power station operators and engineers rely upon a high degree of perceptual skills when they look at displays on instrument panels, and when they check the condition of machinery in the plant itself. Hairdressing requires a very high level of perceptual skills in matching styles to features and personality and in responses to individual clients. Window-dressing, of course, is almost entirely a perceptual–motor skill task of a well-defined kind. Other occupations such as accountancy, economics, professional football or car assembly emphasize either cognitive or motor skills and perception becomes less critical. A qualification to this statement is when accountants have extensive face-to-face dealing with clients. The skills use and performance of most jobs can be influenced by the particular context and this has to be taken into account when analysing needs.

There are some techniques that are particularly suitable for the investigation of perceptual skill. AET allows for the wider view of work and can take account of the ergonomic issues that are most often linked to perceptual skill. Repertory grid, provided that reasonably articulate people can be found, is a sound technique for discovering the perceptions people have of their surroundings. Listening and questioning, when adopted as a technique, can be very effective in uncovering critical parts of perceptual skill use. Where people are reluctant to be too open with others about their perceptions and how they use them, the delphi or nominal group technique can be used.

Different techniques are appropriate depending upon the type of skill being investigated. If you decide to adopt the approaches to learning needs analysis that are recommended in this book, the rationale for linking techniques to skill type will become more apparent as you use the techniques.

Oh yes, you are probably still thinking about the 'F' finding exercise; if you found fewer than six, try again.

9 Investigating knowledge and attitudes

So far we have been investigating various aspects of skills and abilities and how far needs in these areas can be analysed against a backdrop of changing work practices. Whenever skills and abilities are discussed, at some stage there is a reference to the importance of attitudes and also to the need for certain knowledge. It is apparent that some people who are highly skilled and have sound abilities appropriate to the work in hand still fail to meet expectations. It is the two elements of attitude and knowledge that are most often put forward as possible reasons for any failure in this respect. The aim of this chapter is to explore what we mean by work-related attitudes, our use of knowledge, and how far attitudes and knowledge can be accommodated when analysing learning needs.

Self-diagnosis: knowledge

Work-related knowledge can be described in three basic ways:

1. Working knowledge that is needed as an integral part of a task.
2. Accessible knowledge that can be found when you need it.
3. Sporadic use of knowledge.

One of the outcomes of the introduction of the microprocessor, is that most knowledge is now, like water, readily available on tap. However, beer provides a better analogy than water, because you cannot go to any tap, it is necessary to know which tap or source will provide you with what you need. It is then that knowledge about *where* to find knowledge becomes important. In the past few years a new expanding profession of 'knowledge brokers' has developed, particularly in the United States of America. Briefly, their service is designed to provide knowledge about any topic under the sun in minutes or a few hours. As company networking between extensive databases expands, it is likely that this service will be required much less.

Some jobs such as nursing require a high ratio of working knowledge to accessible knowledge. Although the knowledge load on nurses has increased, it still has to be an integral part of their daily tasks. A nurse standing at your bedside consulting a manual is not a comforting sight, yet an aircraft maintenance engineer, who has to deal with electronic complexity, can never be far from sources of accessible knowledge. In this latter type of work, people are generally discouraged from relying too heavily upon knowledge stored in memory.

Some jobs require only very sporadic use of accessible knowledge and this is often quite problematic, because in such circumstances there is normally a lack of knowledge about how to seek out what needs to be known. An example of this is found among highly skilled carpenters who retain an enormous amount of knowledge about how different woods behave and use this knowledge as an integral part of their skilled behaviour. When the need arises to work with a less common wood, such as lignum vitae, then a search for knowledge begins, usually from the brains of various colleagues or contacts.

Can you describe the typical mix of the three knowledge types – working, accessible and sporadic – that exist in the work with which you are familiar? Does the need for knowledge provide problems at any time?

There are, more detailed, ways to think about work-related knowledge than the three broad categories described above. Common in manufacturing industry is **pictorial knowledge**, which is knowing what quality looks like. This knowledge is not always as obvious as it may seem to the outsider; people are told when things do not look right, but there is not necessarily a shared perception among a workforce of what 'right' looks like. Perceptual skills play a significant part in the use of pictorial knowledge, but people still need to know what it is they are asked to perceive, especially when it can include quite acute detail. What is the level of pictorial knowledge in your work and are there any difficulties in satisfying any needs in this respect? Another way of thinking about this issue is to ask, 'What does a quality product or outcome look like in my organization?'

Another type of knowledge is concerned with the order in which tasks are performed; this is **procedural knowledge**. In tasks as simple as making and serving a cup of tea there can be a number of variations to the order in which sub-tasks are performed. Procedural knowledge exists about the way these tasks ought to be performed but whether one person's mental program is more effective than that of another person is open to question. The same comment can be made about almost every task we perform at work. Although the end result of a task undertaken by two different people may be the same, there can be important differences in procedure and one method may be more cost effective than the other. What part does procedural knowledge play in your area of work and are you satisfied that no need exists for knowledge about most effective procedures?

Knowledge about techniques is given prominence in this book, especially how this knowledge can be combined to form an effective strategy for learning needs analysis. Techniques by their nature are often personal to the person practising them – 'Oh, I have my own technique for avoiding this problem' – although periodically some of these techniques slip into general use. A person who has a repertoire of techniques can often respond more flexibly to the changing demands of the workplace than someone who has a limited knowledge of techniques. This is why I class **technique knowledge** as a legitimate form of knowledge in its own right. How many people who are known to you personally, have what you would describe as substantial technique knowledge and can you recognize it as a need in your area of work?

There is almost limitless knowledge about so-called facts, such as all polar bears are left-handed, or water goes down a drain different ways in the northern and southern hemispheres. What we call **factual knowledge** is all around us, from official statistics to 'mastermind' or party game exercises. It is this type of knowledge that is now more extensively on tap than other knowledge. What is your need for this type of knowledge and can your organization access appropriate sources speedily when it is required?

Satisfying the 'need to know' is a vital part of learning needs analysis and this task can be made more fruitful if knowledge itself is better understood. In particular it is important to know which types of knowledge are most affected by changing work practices and which changes demand which type of knowledge.

Self-diagnosis: attitudes

The need for work-related knowledge can be described in ways that are understandable to most people; the same comment cannot be made about attitudes. Many thousands of research hours have been devoted to the study of attitudes, yet as a concept it is of little value in the workplace. Can you give one or more reasons for either agreeing or disagreeing with this statement?

It is very likely that at some time in your working life you have made a comment similar to this: 'You know what the problem is, this group does not have the right attitude.' The key word here is 'attitude' because from this statement it is in attitude that the solution to the 'problem' is felt to lie. In making a comment like this you are assuming at least two things: a) the person you are talking to shares your understanding of the word 'attitude'; and b) the person you are talking to would use the same behaviours that you do in assessing the attitude of the group. If either, or both, of these assumptions do not apply then using the term is a waste of time. People use 'attitude' in the same way as 'initiative' is often used – 'A better attitude is required around here' or 'The manager needs to use more initia-tive'. In both cases the comments are meaningless, unless there is a clear shared perception of what the words 'attitude' and 'initiative' are meant to describe, and in practice this is seldom the case. Can you recall times when you have made comments such as this and been confident that you would be fully understood? Now, upon reflection, can you think of occasions when such comments could have remained unsaid?

A problem when trying to analyse attitude need or attitude change is in knowing what attitude actually is. Originally the term referred to a bodily posture, that is, sitting in a particular attitude, but this meaning is seldom used now. The word has come to mean a state of mind or readiness to respond in a particular way. A more academic definition (Fishbein and Ajzen 1975) is that attitude is 'a learned predisposition to respond in a consistently favourable or unfavourable manner with respect to a given object'. How closely do these attempts to define attitude fit your ideas about the subject?

Attitudes cannot be observed directly; you cannot smell, touch, feel or see attitude. How is it then that organizations talk about changing people's attitudes? The next question is, 'How do *you* assess attitude?

However they are defined, attitudes can only be assessed, if at all, by observing people's various behaviours both verbal and non-verbal. It is questionable whether the results reveal true attitudes or simply what a person wishes you to think of him or her. Can you suggest reasons why this may be the case?

One of the most fruitful ways of looking at attitudes is to think of them as part of a three-way relationship with values and beliefs, as shown in Figure 9.1. Attitudes feed on values and beliefs, and in turn also feed them. All parts of this three-way relationship can be further influenced by knowl-edge as it becomes available. Beliefs are held for various reasons, for example, you may say, 'I believe hanging is appropriate for all murders'; this belief feeds 'an eye for an eye' as a moral principle and standard, which is part of your values. This part of your beliefs and values in turn feeds what can be called a general attitude to the subject of capital punish-ment. Although clues in your behaviour suggest what attitude you hold, the way you behave is influenced by a complex interaction between values, beliefs and attitudes. Can you recognize any implications for analysing attitude need in your organization from this discussion?

The subject of attitudes whether concerning change, need, assessment, or recognition is extremely difficult to handle reliably. Probably the best advice is to examine very carefully whether what you are calling 'attitude' is not better investigated by looking at a particular behaviour of the people concerned.

Investigating knowledge needs

Most of us are reasonably well practised at using equipment, machines or even ideas whilst having little or no knowledge about them. As explained

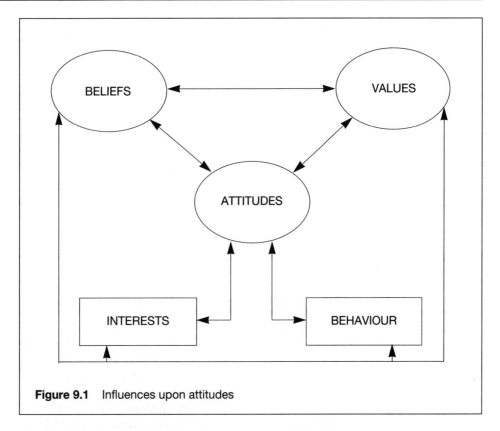

Figure 9.1   Influences upon attitudes

earlier, computers and motor cars are probably the best examples of equipment and machines that can be used on the basis of extremely limited knowledge of the items themselves. In the case of ideas people frequently refer to 'systems' or 'ego' without having any real knowledge about either; as with machines the ideas are used to help us through everyday work and in many cases the lack of knowledge seldom creates difficulties.

In the workplace, a more knowledgeable staff will be referred to as a better educated staff and tends to be seen as an obvious benefit. From the role of 'devil's advocate', such a position can be viewed by the staff concerned as unbeneficial. Knowledge can be associated with thinking, and some people may say they are not paid to think and therefore have no need for further knowledge. From a broader viewpoint, it is often remarked that the people of a certain nation need to have more scientific knowledge and awareness. As in an organization, a clear learning need is being stated without taking account of how individuals perceive the need for such knowledge. The main point here is that it is fruitless to analyse knowledge needs without at the same time including the perceived needs of those who will be involved. At both organizational and national level, there has to be justification for stating such a need. I will pass over the national problem, if there is one, in favour of the more manageable knowledge needs of people in the workplace.

So far, the discussion in this chapter has been rather theoretical, which is almost inevitable because it is very difficult to explain the use of knowledge and attitudes in totally practical terms. Now we will examine some aspects of working practices where knowledge needs do exist at present and then go on to examine attitudes in a similar way.

One area of changing working practice is the move of people from organizations into the home, as discussed in Chapter 5. One expected 'need to know' is how the solitary person best adapts to this new process. An equally important but less obvious knowledge need exists for the people who remain at the office and who must develop new approaches in dealing with the home-based worker. The respective knowledge needs of both groups cannot be adequately investigated separately. Two techniques are particularly useful for bringing the various parties together for the investigation of this type of need: classic brainstorming and nominal group technique (NGT). In this case there are two basic questions: what does each party need to know about the working practice of the other, and what do both need to know about the interrelationships that can arise from the two practices acting together?

The development of automation provides a further example of the effects upon knowledge use of new working patterns. As the use of semi-automated equipment and machinery increases in the workplace, there are indications that people who operate these innovations need to have more knowledge about how they work, in order to perform basic diagnostic tasks, or to enable them to anticipate when problems are about to occur. This applies to people who act as operators in service industries such as banks and shops as well as in manufacturing. The individuals concerned need to be involved in any such investigation from the beginning and must recognize the benefits of acquiring this additional knowledge.

If organizational benefits and individual benefits are not regarded as being the same, the full benefits of this knowledge will seldom be realized. Among western industrialized countries it is the United Kingdom alone where so much distinction is made between organization and management on the one hand and general employees on the other. This leads to the idea of learning needs being of two types: organizational and individual. In other countries there are more moves towards increased cooperation in the workplace, which in turn leads to seeing little or no distinction between individual and organizational needs and benefits. These comments apply equally to skills as well as to knowledge, but apply especially to the gathering of new knowledge. The reason for this is that knowledge can be much more company-specific than skills, and for the individual there may be less perceived benefit to be gained from any transfer of the extra knowledge to another company. In a volatile labour market any new knowledge learning that is strongly company-specific has to be well thought through in terms of how it is identified as a need, and how people are to be involved in the process of recognizing needs in this respect.

As in driving a car or using a computer, some people will use new technology at work without any knowledge about how it works. The response of some investigators is to say that such people have 'no ownership of the technology'; the comment sounds good anyway. However, the individuals concerned need to recognize benefits in having 'ownership', and only they can provide this evidence, with the help of one or two techniques and the help of a facilitator.

This discussion highlights a serious problem in the identification of knowledge need in the workplace. One of the most effective ways of gathering knowledge is by asking questions, and the questioning and listening technique can be conducted with operators to discover what they need to know. However, to be fully effective the operators need to have sufficient knowledge to be able to ask questions in the first place. A useful maxim states 'get someone to do a job and then train them'. This point is emphasized when operators are sent on manufacturers' courses without having first become familiar with the machine or equipment they are to use. Thus they are limited in the questions they can ask and as a result their acquisition of knowledge suffers. An alternative approach to knowledge needs analysis is simply to say, 'What do you know about the working of this equipment?' Generally a more acceptable approach is to ask a few operators to brainstorm as a group all that is known. From this it is often discovered that collectively most of what needs to be known for more effective working practice is already known, but no mechanism exists for the sharing of such knowledge. In other cases some gaps between what is known and what ought to be known can be identified and then floated into the general discussion.

A further aspect of knowledge use at work is the use of knowledge in the learning of skills, and then the practice of skills. It is important to be aware that qualitatively different knowledge may be used in the learning of a skill than in the subsequent performance of the skill on the job. During the learning process the emphasis is usually upon procedural knowledge; later this becomes part of an automatic process and other types of knowledge are used, such as pictorial, accessible, or sporadic.

When learning skills, we make considerable use of knowledge of results (KR) as described in Chapter 6. Knowledge of this kind about how our skill learning is developing, is an essential part of any skills learning.

It is likely that the acquisition and use of factual knowledge will become much less of an issue over the next few years, due to the development of information technology. Other types of knowledge such as procedural, technique and pictorial knowledge will still pose something of a challenge for people who have to analyse learning needs in these areas. One way to demonstrate the type of challenge is to think of the work of knowledge engineers. The work consists mainly of developing knowledge-based systems and expert systems. In the course of this work knowledge is gathered from selected experts in a particular field. Two of the most common fields are medical diagnosis and engineering diagnosis. It is gathering the knowledge about procedures and about perception that causes the greatest difficulties, and a number of techniques are being developed to help people in this task. The person who has to analyse learning needs with respect to knowledge is in a similar position; if you are not fully aware of the different types of knowledge used in a skilled task, how can you analyse the needs of someone who aspires to perform the task? From investigation of work-related knowledge needs it appears that all but factual knowledge will require serious attention, especially as working practices continue to change.

Investigating attitudes at work

It is important to remember that there is no 'right' or 'wrong' attitude in absolute terms. For attitude to be understood at all it has to be talked about in relationship to a specific object, person or event. Also, whether an attitude is seen as favourable or unfavourable depends upon the individuals concerned and most importantly upon the one situation being considered.

Three main components can be identified that make up what we choose to call attitude:

1. The cognitive component.
2. The affective component.
3. The behaviour component.

The cognitive component is an opinion held by a person about a particular subject. For example, the belief that 'People in this place only work for the money' forms part of an attitude towards people's motivation at work.

The affective component is concerned with how people feel about a subject and it can generate much emotion. It can be seen in the statement, 'Choosing people for redundancy in this way is downright unjust'. This component often provides outward indicators of what we call attitude in the emotions of glee, sadness, frustration or anger which it can generate. It is this component that is most difficult to change.

The third component is concerned with what people do – their behaviour. It is how we respond as a result of the opinions and feelings that we hold. People may think that if we know a person's attitude it is possible to predict their behaviour. Unfortunately, human beings do not behave consistently.

An example of the behaviour component would be a protest meeting organized about the planned felling of trees. If there was consistency between the three components of attitude everyone in support of the meeting would believe that the needs of conservation take priority over development and would feel that destroying nature is a criminal act. This would be roughly their cognitive and affective stances. In reality some people in support of the meeting may not hold these views and could be in support for entirely different reasons unconnected with conservation – for example, they may be losing privacy as a result of the trees being felled. Therefore it is impossible to understand behaviour from attitudes alone; we need to know full details of the particular situation.

The same applies to attitude use at work. It is not unknown for managers to behave in a way totally contradictory to that indicated by their attitude. This is also applicable to any one of the other components. A person's feelings about a subject may be lukewarm yet their stated beliefs and certain actions can give the impression that this is a serious subject to them. When seeking to analyse learning needs as a means of changing attitudes we need to ask which of these components are being affected – all or only one or two?

An extensive piece of research in the USA (La Piere 1934), which has spawned other research works with similar results, helps us recognize how behaviour and attitude can be at odds with each other. The researcher travelled widely in the USA in the company of two middle-aged Chinese people and recorded visits to 251 hotels and restaurants. On only one occasion did they encounter difficulty because of ethnic status. Six months after each visit, La Piere sent questions to the establishments concerned asking about their policy towards oriental customers. 92 per cent responded that they would not serve Chinese customers. As a control, the same questions were sent to 100 other establishments at random and similar results were found. The general attitude to serving oriental people was in sharp contrast to the behaviour demonstrated.

Despite the fact that many people in organizations believe that attitude influences behaviour and that behaviour can be predicted from attitude the conclusion has to be that knowledge about attitude does not generally serve these purposes.

One approach by some organizations is to deal with attitude head-on and commission the design and use of attitude surveys. There are serious problems connected with survey questionnaires, but the problems are further compounded when questions are asked about attitudes. Most questionnaires used in surveys of this kind tell us more about the attitude of the people who design the questionnaire than that of the respondents. The main reason for this is that in framing the closed or semi-closed questions it is the concerns as perceived by the question designers that feature most, or at best, the concerns of a so-called representative sample of people used in the piloting of the survey. Extensive research is necessary if such design bias is to be avoided and this is outside the scope of most organizations.

The alternative is to produce a critical incident questionnaire, but this is often too time consuming to be handled well in the work situation. It appears that there is no easy or reliable way to analyse attitudes accurately; in most cases the task becomes one of inference and 'a wet finger in the air' approach. Various attempts to 'measure' attitudes in a scientific way can so often be held up to ridicule.

An approach worth trying is simply to ask people face-to-face what is their attitude to a subject. Then observe verbal and non-verbal behaviour to check for consistency between attitude and behaviour. This simple method can be further facilitated by using Lewin's force field technique. Explain the idea of the technique to a group of people concerned and ask them to draw their own view of a situation. Hospital staff could be asked to think about the changes in the way some mentally disabled people are being cared for in the community. Asking staff to produce their view of what is driving and what is restraining such change, provides insight into what they believe, what they feel and what could be done about the issue. A sharing of the results from such an exercise would go some way towards understanding attitudes that exist, but again, will only make sense when assessed with other knowledge about the developing situation.

One of the main reasons for linking attitude to learning needs is that people in organizations sometimes feel that attitudes must be changed, and that such change can be achieved by shifts in the kind of knowledge given to the workforce and the use of learning programmes. Often the prevailing attitude is thought to be unfavourable and needs to be changed to one that is favourable. Sometimes it is not that an old attitude is unfavourable but that it is no longer appropriate to the changed circumstances. Attempts to change attitude are not necessarily wrong, but a lack of current discussion about the ethics of attitude change is disturbing. Given that what we know about attitudes suggests strongly that they are based upon people's beliefs and values, we have to ask whether anyone has the moral right to change the attitude of another person. It is common for people in industry to speak glibly about attitude change and cultural change, but this is a further example of the fact that people can use ideas like they use equipment and machines – with very little or no real knowledge about them. We also need to question whether attitudes are a relevant part of a learning needs analysis exercise. If it can be demonstrated that unfavourable attitudes are at least partly responsible for any poor performance, then there is justification for looking at learning needs as one means of rectifying the problem.

Before any attempt is made to link attitude to learning needs, sufficient evidence about unfavourable attitude is required, yet there are no clear ways to provide reliable evidence of this. Possibly the most effective approach is to eliminate all other factors that can account for poor performance before turning to attitudes as a last resort. Thus, as a result of using part 1 of the AET technique, are working conditions a possible factor? From a protocol, or critical incident investigation, are there indications of certain skills or knowledge need? From a force field investigation, do people understand significant changes that could be taking place? From what is known about listening and questioning, is there clear evidence that people are listened to? Where team-working is involved, is there evidence of adverse influence upon perceptions from within the group? These and other questions can be asked in order to provide evidence for the elimination of many competing factors, before you turn to the subject of attitudes.

Probably the most important reason for treating attitudes in this way is that attitudes are symptoms rather than causes. In other words, if you suspect attitude to be a 'problem', then deal with it as a symptom and look for the true causes of the problem.

10 Taking a wide view of learning needs

Self-diagnosis

A large amount of literature on the subject of training needs analysis includes recommendations to base training needs, whenever possible, upon business plan information. However, there is a shortage of advice about how to link business planning to training needs analysis. How does your organization link learning needs to knowledge gained from business plans?

Although a business plan is normally a single document there are at least three parts to business planning; these can be crudely described as short, medium and long term. Can you recognize which business plans in your experience fall into these three categories, and are different terms used to describe them?

People in a company who are responsible for analysing training needs, or, in the terminology of this book, learning needs, need access to business plan information. Can you identify the people in your organization who have knowledge of business plan information, and do any of these people analyse learning needs?

Some people believe that business planning is basically about strategy and prefer to use the term strategic planning. Can you identify which activities in your organization best provide examples of strategic planning?

Another view of strategic planning is that the term is a contradiction; planning is a formal well-structured process and strategy includes a strong element of creativeness, and the two do not live very well together. People who hold this view say that strategic thinking, which can involve some creativity, occurs first and then the outcome of this process is used during business planning. What is your view on this difference between strategy and planning?

An important ingredient of business planning is the decision as to which time-scale to adopt – does a plan cover months or years? What is the time-scale of the business plan in your own organization? Is this time-scale realistic?

If you are confident that the analysis of learning needs in your organization is based, even partly, on sound business plan information, then you need only to skim through this chapter to discover whether there are any useful points to note. If, on the other hand, your response to some of these diagnostic questions has been to scratch your head or ask, 'What business plan?' then a full reading of this chapter will be of value to you.

Background

This chapter concerns what you need to know in order to take a wide view of learning needs in your organization, and in particular to help you make the essential link between business planning and the analysis of learning needs. Although closely related to other parts of the book, a shift of emphasis is made from the analysis of knowledge, skills and abilities, to thinking about how these aspects of human performance can be related to business planning, and vice versa. Incidentally, the word 'business' is used here to include any value-adding activity that can be described as occupational. Some confusion can arise in areas such as education or the voluntary sector, where people may not think that they are involved in business, but using the definition given here they clearly are. In fact, the voluntary sector in some countries is now rivalling manufacturing as a source of value-adding occupations.

Another point to clarify is that the chapter does not include details about how to conduct business planning – there are a number of excellent textbooks on the subject already. Its aims are to show how existing business plans can be used as a means of analysing learning needs in advance of requirement, so that needs analysis and fulfilment can also be planned. In order to do this, however, we first need to establish the main elements of business planning, especially those that may provide a clue to future needs.

Controversy exists about the level of openness in business. People who are involved in the analysis of learning needs are most often found in the supervisory or middle-manager level of organizations, and may not have access to business plan information. In such circumstances recommendations about using this information to analyse needs cannot be implemented. In the United Kingdom, recommendations for greater cooperation and openness in organizations were made almost twenty years ago (Bullock 1977). While in some western industrialized countries, in particular Germany, such cooperation and openness has developed, progress from autocracy to democracy in the UK, in response to the Bullock Report, has been slow.

What is at issue is the 'climate' of an organization. Climate is most clearly identified through observable signs from people's behaviour and procedures that reflect general custom and practice. The analysis of learning needs is influenced by the particular climate that prevails within a company.

One sign of climate can be recognized by looking at the flow of information. If there is little flow of information, then learning needs may well be difficult to establish clearly because anticipation of what has to be done, and what has to be known, is not likely to be common knowledge.

Another indication of climate can be that people are readily blamed for any problems that occur. This is a 'climate of blame' in which people feel reluctant to try any new ideas and as a result learning tends to be avoided. The word 'blame' could, perhaps, be banned from the English language; it is negative, always destructive and never constructive. If you operate in a climate of blame it is highly likely that the analysis of learning needs will be a difficult task.

Incidently, a clear distinction is being made here between climate and culture. In contrast to climate, culture cannot be observed because it is concerned with fundamental beliefs and values that people collectively hold within an organization. Reference has been made already to the question of the moral validity of trying to change people's attitudes and the question is much more critical in terms of beliefs and values. In general it is healthier to work within a particular culture and change only the climate, that is, how people perform tasks and the general procedures that are adopted. This issue of climate recognition should be kept in mind when planning for needs analysis. If analysing learning needs is found to be difficult, the causes may well lie with climate-related factors.

Business planning

Before we examine how business plan information can be used in the analysis of learning needs it may be helpful to clarify the various parts of business planning, and to relate each part to the process of needs analysis.

There are three main elements of business planning and each one differs from the others in terms of time-scale and emphasis. Working from the shortest time-scale to the longest, we have first what is called operational planning, where the time-scale is in days and weeks; the emphasis is on fine level of detail about day-to-day activities such as stores control, staffing, costs and observing birthdays. At the other extreme is long-term strategic planning.

The intermediate section of planning which falls between the short-term operational work and the longer term strategic planning is most often referred to as management planning, but here it will be called diagnostic planning. There are two main reasons for this change in emphasis. One reason is that it is not always managers who are involved in this part of the planning process; technicians, designers, team-leaders and planners themselves can each play the leading role. The second reason is that diagnosis best describes what actually happens, and is in line with the terms operational and strategic which also describe the essence of the activities in their respective parts of planning. At this intermediate stage the time-scale normally covers months. The main aim is to provide a link between strategic planning and operational planning. This link is made through a diagnosis of strategic information and relevant findings are fed into the operational stage. Then diagnosis of the operational stage activities contributes to the deliberations that make up strategic planning, that is, the strategic thinking. The gap between the content of strategic planning and operational planning is normally too great for any meaningful links to be made in a direct way, so the diagnosis is vital and it is here that the analysis of learning needs ought to take place.

The third and final part of business planning is known as strategic planning which, when done well, is divided between strategic thinking and planning. The time-scale for strategic planning is normally one year or more, up to a maximum of five years. A strategic plan of two years can be quite acceptable to many companies and up to five years shows an increasing level of confidence in being able to project likely business activity. A company that plans beyond five years would require a large degree of control over its environment. The emphasis of strategic planning is upon wide company aims and objectives; such as product and/or service development, market share, budget, capital investment, utilization of technology and innovation.

A contradiction can be seen in the use of the term 'operational planning'. What is called planning at the operational stage would appear to be too late and the cynic would call it fire-fighting, however, the reality of the hustle and bustle of industrial life dictates that last minute planning becomes an important part of the overall plan. Ideally, the planning for operational activities should take place at the diagnosis stage and the function of the operational stage is to carry out the plan rather than undertake planning as an integral part of operational work. For this approach to function properly diagnosis planning must be regarded as a high profile activity. In organizations where this does happen, analysis of learning needs is made easier.

In the discussion about different parts of planning, there are important implications for the analysis of learning needs. First, while learning needs may emerge from operational planning, the analysis of learning needs will not be effective as a routine operational activity; any analysis of need at this stage is too late and leads to rushed and ineffective learning. This is why learning needs should be based upon business plan information and in particular the strategic part of planning.

It is not realistic to expect the analysis of learning needs to be included in strategic business planning, but having said this, more attention could be given to knowledge, skills and abilities as part of strategic thinking. The analysis of learning needs should form part of diagnostic planning. A diagnosis of the strategic plan can produce ideas and clues that help predict which knowledge, skills and abilities will be needed in the future. This task has not been well described in the literature but some useful methods will be provided later in this chapter. When the task of analysing learning needs from a strategic plan is complete, a diagnosis of the operational activities can be made to determine whether a gap exists between learning requirements that have emerged from the strategic plan and the availability of knowledge, skills and abilities among the current workforce.

There are other implications for the analysis of learning needs; in particular, the idea that information from the operational stage will be mainly concerned with learning for improvement, that is, learning to improve the level of knowledge and skills in order to improve overall performance. Information from the strategic stage is more likely to indicate the need for new knowledge and skills and possibly the use of some abilities not previously used. The call to learn new skills and knowledge as opposed to 'learn for improvement' is more likely to occur when the strategic plan includes objectives to have new products and/or services, or an increase in the level of innovation. The difference between operational and strategic information described here is only one of emphasis. Operational information can still lead to the need for new knowledge and skills and possibly abilities, while strategic information can point to areas where improved knowledge and skills are required.

Another implication for learning needs analysis which comes from an exploration of business planning is the issue of time-scales. If the learning need has been identified in a reactive way as a result of a new practice being adopted at the operational stage, then it has been identified too late. However, identification of a learning need too early can be as damaging as identifying it too late. If the need is identified too early, and acted upon, a time gap can exist between learning and an opportunity to practise the new or improved knowledge and skills. Direct work-related practice must be available to people immediately following any programme of learning. Another problem in this respect is that identification of need can build up in people an expectation that some learning opportunity is to be offered. Identification too early can lead to frustration or loss of interest when the proposed action for learning is delayed. The accurate timing of identification and of learning need fulfilment relies heavily upon strategic information; without an advanced indication of when initiatives are required it is not possible adequately to plan any learning programme.

The next issue concerns who ought to have access to strategic information. In some organizations the professionals who are given the responsibility for training, and anything that relates to learning, have a low profile. If the role is looked upon in this way it is almost inevitable that such people will act in accordance with the expectations of the role, that is, do as instructed and behave in a reactive manner. If an organization is to be a learning organization, someone at director or senior manager level must diagnose strategic plan information for the purpose of extracting information relevant to learning needs to pass on to those at supervisory or middle manager level. With access to information of this kind, it is possible for people at this level in the organization to interpret it in terms of anticipated learning needs. The task of locating this relevant strategic information, and the analysis of needs is covered in the next section.

Identifying and making use of strategic information

It is rare for anything more than a passing reference to knowledge and skills needs to be included in the body of a business plan. Seldom is a clear statement or section included that could be extracted and given to someone with responsibility for learning needs identification. Even where clues are provided it is not commonly within the remit of business plan writing to include such details.

There are two stages to using strategic plan information for the purpose of analysing learning needs:

1. Location of proposed actions within the plan that may have implications for learning needs. All actions that could have the slightest implications are highlighted; they can be dropped later if no need exists.
2. A detailed examination of the proposed actions, using techniques and applying what is known about different types of knowledge, skill and ability.

The first stage of locating relevant actions involves an overview of the strategic plan. Two techniques detailed in Chapter 5 are helpful here: storyboard and SWOT analysis. In practice most business plans can be described pictorially and storyboard is a good way to achieve this. In the first box of storyboard a picture is drawn of how the plan describes the current business activities; in the last box a picture shows what the activities of the business are expected to look like at the end of the plan's timespan. The remaining boxes are completed to show the activities that are needed in order to achieve the stated aims and objectives.

The storyboard technique allows you to stand back and see whether implications for learning need immediately spring to mind. Business activities that do appear in this way can be recorded immediately. A deeper examination of the storyboard is then needed to see how far relevant activities can be inferred from the pictures – what is being suggested here that can have a knock-on effect to learning needs? The technique is used to best advantage when two to three people can share ideas and promote inspiration. However, the approach can be used by only one senior person who has full access to the strategic plan. We saw earlier that strategic working normally involves some element of creativity and the storyboard technique provides an opportunity to exercise creative thinking.

The other appropriate technique is SWOT analysis, as described in Chapter 5. Like classic brainstorming, SWOT analysis has become well known in organizations over the past twenty years or so. While the technique is straightforward to use, some thought is needed in interpreting the results, depending upon the particular context in which the technique is being applied. The first task is to write down in the appropriate boxes all the strengths, weaknesses, opportunities and threats that can be gathered from exploration of the strategic plan. When this has been completed, a useful start to the analysis is to identify which weaknesses can be re-framed into strengths. The statement, 'It is not likely that staff in Plant D will have the necessary skills to adapt to the proposed change in technology use', can be re-framed as 'The staff in Plant D are in a position to learn new knowledge and skills in readiness for the introduction of new technology.' Re-framing is a simple technique to provide a different perspective on a subject.

An alternative approach to the identified weaknesses of the organization is to think of ways to avoid them. However, weakness avoidance is not to be recommended as a means of analysing learning needs; effective learning concerns knowing how to do things well, rather than how to avoid doing things badly, or learning how to avoid weaknesses. The only valid approach to identified weaknesses is either to re-frame them or meet them head-on with corrective actions. When all weaknesses that can be re-framed are included in the box of strengths, the next task is to see how far the strengths can be either built upon or better utilized by additional learning.

The next step in the SWOT analysis is to examine the threats which have possible implications for learning needs. One example from a strategic plan might be, 'The growth of television-watching is a significant threat to our cinema business.' The statement can be re-framed to read, 'The growth of television usage provides us with an opportunity and a need to think of ways to develop the cinema experience so that it becomes more appealing than home-based entertainment.' Such re-framing can produce implications for the knowledge and skill need of cinema management and staff. The stated threat has been re-framed as an opportunity. When as many threats as possible have been processed in this way, the now complete list of opportunities can be considered.

One main aim of a SWOT analysis is to see how far opportunities can be maximized – what can people in the organization do to take full advantage of the identified opportunities? In a comprehensive strategic plan that highlights opportunities there ought to be statements of intentions that will lead to some form of opportunity-taking. In order to maximize opportunities all possible initiatives that could be taken should be listed, even those that seem bizarre. Within such statements there lie, almost inevitably, implications for learning needs. Typically, needs arise from proposed initiatives in the following way:

- There are clear indications that we need to increase the market awareness of our staff.
- To become more readily receptive to sudden orders, a selective use of dual skilling will be necessary.

- The contract team on site has to operate as an autonomous unit in future; there is a need for members to be familiar with logistic planning.
- Feedback from clients indicates we have some lack of current knowledge. Sales personnel need more product up-dates.
- The current sensing units are reaching the end of their useful life and within six months it is intended to invest in new technology.
- Two possible client groups have been identified, but we have no experience in this part of the market.

These statements share a common concern about the need to exploit opportunities; each has implications for the analysis of learning needs.

The use of storyboard and/or SWOT analysis provides insight into strategic planning information in a way that leads to the initial identification of proposed activities that require learning of some kind to take place.

Although an aim throughout this book has been to avoid the check-list approach to learning needs analysis, it is appropriate at this stage to list some examples of typical activities quoted in a business plan that indicate the existence of implications for learning needs. These are listed in Figure 10.1. Other activity statements can be found in a comprehensive strategic plan, but those listed are typical examples of statements that strongly suggest implications for learning needs.

When activity statements, similar to those above, have been generated from the plan it is helpful to use a modified and short version of the critical incident technique for the purpose of prioritizing them in terms of learning needs. The senior person conducting this investigation should be in a position to determine which activities will have the greatest impact upon business performance and therefore require further investigation to describe the precise learning needs, and whether any further learning is necessary for activities to take place. Using the principle of the critical incident technique at this stage means that the most important activities will be targeted first. The work of the senior manager or director is now complete, and all activities that have been gathered from the strategic plan will be available

---

- The development of new products and/or services
- To expand (or reduce) current markets
- To develop new markets
- A proposed entry into a market new to the company
- To have more effective utilization of suppliers
- To introduce a new management development programme
- To reconsider recruitment policy
- To seek more opportunities for creativity and innovation
- To make better use of existing resources
- To shift the balance between the use of core and peripheral employees
- To promote the adoption of more new technology

Figure 10.1 Business activities that can prompt learning needs

as a statement of prioritized implications for learning needs over the life-span of the plan.

The next stage is concerned with a more detailed investigation of the prioritized implications. It is conducted by someone with an understanding of the different types of knowledge, skill and ability, and who also knows something of the process of learning. The first step is to look at the main priority, which may be, for example, developing a new product. This initial exploration almost inevitably involves some searching for information, in particular who can be expected to be involved in the whole development process from design through production to implementation. For each category of people questions should be asked about the types of knowledge, skill and ability that will be required. For those who will be involved in production, the knowledge need may include knowing about a new material, how it behaves and how it is joined during the process. The skills may be identified as being confined to programming and operating a robot-operated system. Five abilities may be applicable: finger dexterity, manual dexterity, number facility, problem sensitivity, and deductive reasoning. When this information has been gathered it is a good idea to ask for constructive criticism from those who have a deep understanding of the process, such as designers, outside suppliers or in-house technical personnel.

The next step is to compare the knowledge, skills and abilities that will be required, with those available among the existing workforce. The best approach at this stage is to see whether the abilities that have been identified as necessary are used in the performance of existing jobs. If a reasonably close match can be established between the abilities currently practised and those required, some confidence can be felt that any programme of re-training or provision of other learning such as job-aids, shadowing or open learning will produce effective results quite rapidly. A similar approach is used finally to highlight any gap that may exist between available knowledge and what will be required. Collectively this information represents a clear statement of learning needs. If the required abilities are largely absent among the workforce, two questions need to be asked:

1. Are any of the required abilities difficult to improve through programmes of learning?
2. How realistic is it to recruit people with the necessary abilities?

If the answer to the first question if 'Yes', then serious difficulties may be experienced by people who are required to learn the new production process. If you think back to the discussion about abilities in Chapter 2 you will realize that if the five abilities listed above have already been demonstrated in the current work it is unlikely that any serious problems will be experienced in learning the newly required skills. On the other hand, if the abilities of colour discrimination, rate control or visualization feature in the requirements, a more serious investigation of how the skills are to be provided will be needed. The choice may lie between an elaborate programme of learning or the buying-in of the skills.

A wider view of this matching of required knowledge and skills to available knowledge and skills can be demonstrated by examples from a government's strategic plan and a similar organization plan. If the United Kingdom government decided to replace two nuclear power stations that were being decommissioned, or an oil company decided to open up a new offshore field, there would be a gap between the high level fabrication and welding skills that would be required and the availability of such skills. Work on these projects could be in progress before it was realized that such a gap existed. However, an analysis of learning needs at the operational stage would be fruitless because such an advanced level of skills cannot be learnt over a short period of time and the likely solution would be to use imported skills. The analysis of such learning needs would have to be planned in advance and worked upon at the diagnosis stage of business planning.

Summary

It can be seen from this discussion that strategic business plans can provide a rich source of information that is directly relevant to the task of analysing learning needs. Ideally the people in an organization who are responsible for this task should have access to the strategic plan so that they can identify and extract blocks of information that are relevant to learning needs. Some senior management involvement will probably be required to help prioritize the activities and initiatives that have been extracted from the plan. The next step is to identify all the implications that exist for how people behave, in connection with the use of knowledge, skills and the role of attitudes.

Techniques drawn from Chapters 4 and 5 or from your own experience, can be used to help analyse more closely the types of knowledge, skill and ability that will be required, and when they will be required. It is important at this stage to disregard current uses of skills, knowledge and abilities. The reason is that the emphasis has to be upon what *will* be needed, and the inclusion of any information about current unfulfilled needs can confuse the analysis.

When future learning needs have been analysed in this way, each set of needs can be clearly set out to include the following items:

- Statement of the initial initiative/proposal/plan that prompted the anticipation of needs.
- The stated level of priority given by senior personnel.
- A summary of technique-based analysis, listing the types of skill, knowledge and ability that will be required.
- A statement about any anticipated difficulties in meeting the needs, based upon abilities requirement and knowledge of the labour market.

- An analysis of the learning that will be required to fulfil the skills and/or knowledge needs, and any special learning needs to overcome weaknesses in abilities.

Using this information, a comparison can be made with current use of skills, knowledge and abilities in the target areas of the organization. Keep an open mind about people in the workforce: the skills and knowledge being demonstrated by people at the current time are not necessarily a true reflection of their capabilities. In this respect, people ought to have the means to make prior skills and knowledge known to the organization. If it has been possible to involve people in the application of one or two techniques to analyse learning needs, they will be more receptive to finding ways to meet needs identified from the business plan. Otherwise, opportunities need to be created for people to check through the projected learning needs in order to assess how far they will be prepared to go in learning any new skills and/or knowledge. When knowledge of projected abilities requirements is made known, people are in a better position to assess how near they are to meeting the requirements. This is done by comparing these abilities with those that they are already using. When it can be shown that someone is not starting from first principles in learning a new skill or in accumulating new knowledge, this can provide encouragement to learn.

Throughout this book, I have been optimistic that organizations will become more open and less status conscious in order to meet more flexibly the demands of rapidly changing technology. This view may be too idealistic, but divided strata in organizations, in which only certain people are fully involved, will not survive the changes in technology. The techniques and approaches that this book offers demand cooperation and openness throughout an organization.

References

Asch, S.E. (1956) 'Studies of independence and conformity. A minority of one against a unanimous majority', *Psychological Monographs* 70 (9).

Bloomer, C.M. (1976) *Principles of Visual Perception*, London: The Herbert Hill Press.

Bullock, A. (1977) *Report of the Committee of Inquiry on Industrial Democracy. Department of Trade and Industry*. London: HMSO.

Burley-Allen, M. (1982) *Listening: The Forgotten Skill*, Chichester: Wiley.

Craig, M. (1985) 'Selection testing', *Training and Development Journal*, January.

Downs, S. (1992) 'Learning to Learn' in S. Truelove. (ed.) *Handbook of Training and Development*, Oxford: Blackwell Business.

Ericsson, K.A. and Simon, H. (1985) *Protocol Analysis, Verbal Reports as Data*, London: MIT Press.

Fishbein, M. and Ajzen, I. (1975), *Belief, Intention, Attitude and Behaviour: An Introduction to Theory and Research*, Reading Mass.: Addison-Wesley.

Fitts, P.M. and Jones, R.E. (1947) 'Reduction of pilot error by design of aircraft controls', *Air Technical Intelligence (ATI) Technical Data Digest*, 12 (4): 4–20.

Fivars, G. (1980) *Bibliography of 700 Critical Incident Technique Studies*, Palo Alto: American Institute for Research.

Flanagan, J.C. (1954) 'The critical incident technique', *The Psychological Bulletin* 51 (4).

Fleishman, E.A. (1982) 'Systems for describing human tasks', *American Psychologist* 37 (7): 821–34.

Gregory, R. (1966) *Eye and Brain*, London: World University Library.

Holt, K. (1991) 'What is the best way to organise projects?' in J. Henry and D. Walker (eds) *Managing Innovation*, London: Open University and Sage Publications.

Kelly, G.A. (1985) *The Psychology of Personal Constructs*, New York: W.W. Norton.

Labaw, P.J. (1980) *Advances in Questionnaire Design*, Cambridge, Mass.: Abt Books.

La Piere, R.T. (1934) 'Attitudes versus actions', *Social Forces* 13: 230–7.

Linstone, H.A. and Turoff, M. (1977) *The Delphi Method, Techniques and Applications*, Reading, Mass.: Addison-Wesley.

MacKay, I. (1980) *A Guide to Asking Questions*, London: BACIE.

MacKay, I. (1984) *A Guide to Listening*, London: BACIE.

MacKay, I. (1989) *Expecting Answers*, London: BACIE.

Majaro, S. (1988) *The Creative Gap*, London: Longman.

Osborn, A.F. (1963) *Applied Imaginations*, New York: Scribner.

Reeves, T.K. and Harper, D. (1981) *Surveys at Work, A Practitioners Guide*, London: McGraw-Hill.

Rohmert, W. and Landau, K. (1983) *Ergonomic Job Analysis*, London: Taylor Francis.

Scott, D. and Deadrick, D. (1982) 'The nominal group technique: applications for training needs assessment', *Training and Development Journal*, June, 26–33.

Steil, L.K. (1983) *Listening*, Chichester: Wiley.

Stewart, V. (1981) *Business Applications of Repertory Grid*, London: McGraw-Hill.

Toffler, A. (1971) *Future Shock*, London: Pan.

Van de Ven, A.H. and Delbecq, A.L. (1971) 'Nominal versus interacting group processes for committee decision-making effectiveness', *Academy of Management Journal*, June, 203–12.

Van Gundy, A.B. (1988) *Techniques of Structured Problem Solving*, New York: Van Nostrand Reinhold.

Recommended reading

Bailey, R.W. (1989) *Human Performance Engineering*, Murray Hill, NJ: Prentice-Hall International Inc.

Baltes, P.B. and Baltes, M.M. (1990) *Successful Ageing*, Cambridge: CUP.

Fleishman, E.A. and Quaintance, M.K. (1984) *Taxonomies of Human Performance*, Orlando: Academic Press.

Gael, S. (1988) *Job Analysis Handbook for Business Industry and Government*, 2 vols, New York: John Wiley & Sons.

Kragt, H. (1992) *Enhancing Industrial Performance*, London: Taylor and Francis.

McCormack, B. and Kenefick, D. (1991) *Learning on the Job*, London: Souvenir Press (E&A) Ltd.

Stanfer, M.C. (1992) 'Technological change and the older employee', *Behaviour and Information Technology* 11 (1): 46–52.

Index

A Handbook for Training Strategy

Martyn Sloman

The traditional approach to training in the organization is no longer effective. That is the central theme of Martyn Sloman's challenging book. A new model is required that will reflect the complexity of organizational life, changes in the HR function and the need to involve line management. This Handbook introduces such a model and describes the practical implications not only for human resource professionals and training managers but also for line managers.

Martyn Sloman writes as an experienced training manager and his book is concerned above all with implementation. Thus his text is supported by numerous questionnaires, survey instruments and specimen documents. It also contains the findings of an illuminating survey of best training practice carried out among UK National Training Award winners.

The book is destined to make a significant impact on the current debate about how to improve organizational performance. With its thought-provoking argument and practical guidance it will be welcomed by everyone with an interest in the business of training and development.

Contents

1994	240 pages	0 566 07393 5

Gower

Making the Most of Action Learning

Scott Inglis

Here at last is a book on action learning designed to be read by non-specialists. Drawing extensively on case histories and "real life" examples, the author:

- describes what action learning is and how it works
- shows how to bring action learning into an organization
- discusses the benefits to be expected and the costs involved
- explains how to avoid common pitfalls.

Unlike much of the existing material on action learning, the emphasis here is on the needs of the organization, whether in the private or the public sector. The main model used is that of an in-house action learning programme designed to tackle issues of critical importance to the organization.

For any manager wanting to know what action learning can do for his or her organization, Scott Inglis's new book is the ideal guide.

Contents

1994   256 pages   0 566 07452 4

Gower

Participative Training Skills

John Rodwell

It is generally accepted that, for developing skills, participative methods are the best. Here at last is a practical guide to maximizing their effectiveness.

Drawing on his extensive experience as a trainer, John Rodwell explores the whole range of participative activities from the trainer's point of view. The first part of his book looks at the principles and the "core skills" involved. It shows how trainee participation corresponds to the processes of adult learning and goes on to describe each specific skill, including the relevant psychological models. The second part devotes a chapter to each method, explaining:

- what it is
- when and why it is used
- how to apply the core skills in relation to the method
- how to deal with potential problems.

A "skills checklist" summarizes the guidelines presented in the chapter. The book ends with a comprehensive matrix showing which method is most suitable for meeting which objectives.

For anyone concerned with skill development *Participative Training Skills* represents an invaluable handbook.

Contents

1994   192 pages   0 566 07444 3

Gower

Teambuilding Strategy

Mike Woodcock and Dave Francis

There is no doubt that working through teams can be an effective way to accomplish tasks in an organization. As Woodcock and Francis point out, though, it is by no means the only one. Managers concerned with human resource strategy cannot afford to assume that teamwork will always be the best option. A number of questions need to be asked before any decision is made, such as:

- what should be the focus of our organization development interventions?
- should we undertake teambuilding initiatives?
- how extensive should the teambuilding initiative be?
- what resources will we need to support our teambuilding initiative?

This book provides a framework within which these questions may be addressed. It presents a structured approach to analysing the key issues, including a series of questionnaires and activities designed to guide the reader through the key strategic decisions that must be taken by any organization contemplating a teambuilding programme. The authors, two of the best known specialists in the field, examine the benefits and dangers of teambuilding as an organization development strategy and offer detailed guidance on further information and resources.

This is the second and considerably reworked edition of *Organisation Development Through Teambuilding*, first published in 1982.

Contents

1994   160 pages   0 566 07496 6

Training Needs Analysis
A Resource for Identifying Training Needs, Selecting Training Strategies, and Developing Training Plans

Sharon Bartram and Brenda Gibson

This unique manual is designed as a practical tool for trainers. It contains 22 instruments and documents for gathering and processing information about training and development issues within your organization. This frees you from the time-consuming business of formulating methods for generating information and allows you to concentrate instead on the all-important task of making contacts and building relationships.

Part I of the manual examines the process of identifying and analysing training needs. It reviews the different types of information the instruments will generate and provides guidance on deciding how training needs can best be met. This part concludes with ideas for presenting training plans and making your findings and proposals acceptable to others.

Part II contains the instruments themselves. They cover organizational development, organizational climate, managing resources and job skills. Each section begins with an introduction which defines the area covered, describes the instruments, and identifies the target groups. It also provides a checklist of the preparations you will need to make. The instruments themselves represent a wide range of methods, including card sorts, questionnaires, profiles and grids.

Effective training requires a serious investment in time and finance. This manual will help you to ensure that the investment your organization makes will achieve the desired results.

Contents
Preface • Introduction • Part I Analysing Training Needs • Part II The Instruments • Section One Developing the organization• Section Two Organization climate • Section Three Managing Resources • Section Four Job Skills.

1994   160 pages   0 566 07561 X Hardback   0 566 07437 0 Looseleaf

Gower